Class, Critics, and Shakespeare

D0885933

Class, Critics, and Shakespeare
Bottom Lines on the Culture Wars

SHARON O'DAIR

Ann Arbor
THE UNIVERSITY OF MICHIGAN PRESS

Copyright © by the University of Michigan 2000
All rights reserved
Published in the United States of America by
The University of Michigan Press
Manufactured in the United States of America
⊗ Printed on acid-free paper

2003   2002   2001   2000   4   3   2   1

A CIP catalog record for this book is available from the British Library.

Library of Congress Cataloging-in-Publication Data

O'Dair, Sharon.
    Class, critics, and Shakespeare : bottom lines on the culture wars
  / Sharon O'Dair.
       p.   cm.
    Includes bibliographical references (p.   ) and index.
    ISBN 0-472-09754-7 (alk. paper) — ISBN 0-472-06754-0 (pbk. : alk.
  paper)
    1. Shakespeare, William, 1564–1616—Criticism and
  interpretation—History—20th century.   2. Shakespeare, William,
  1564–1616—Study and teaching—United States.   3. Shakespeare,
  William, 1564–1616—Appreciation—United States.   4. Culture—Social
  aspects—United States—History—20th century.   5. Literature and
  society—United States—History—20th century.   6. Social
  classes—United States—History—20th century.   7. Criticism—United
  States—History—20th century.   I. Title.
  PR2970 .O34   2000
  822.3'3—dc21   00-09805

Dedicated, with thanks and love,
to the memory of my mother, Edna O'Dair,
and to the memory of my father, Wes O'Dair

Acknowledgments

O ne of the pleasures of finishing this book is gaining the opportunity to thank for their support a number of friends, colleagues, and institutions. The University of Alabama provided sabbatical leave and a summer research grant in 1995, during which time I began work in earnest on this project. Sara deSaussure Davis, chair in the Department of English at Alabama, has created an excellent environment for intellectual work. The English department funded the fine work done by Abigail Scherer, my research assistant during 1997–98. Thanks also is due to the Humanities Center at the University of Oregon, where for six weeks in the summer of 1995, I used both archival and first-hand sources to develop the ideas that became "Shakespeare in the Woods." Kathleen Leary, archivist at the Oregon Shakespeare Festival, located documents necessary to complete that essay, and the Humanities Center brought me back to Eugene in 1998 to read it to a critical and knowledgeable audience. The University of Michigan Press's anonymous readers also subjected the manuscript to detailed and pressured critique, which I have tried to satisfy in revising the manuscript.

Portions of this book first appeared in different form: as "Beyond Necessity: The Consumption of Class, the Production of Status, and the Persistence of Inequality" in *New Literary History* 31.2 (2000): 337–53; as "The Status of Class in Shakespeare; or, Why Critics Love to Hate Capitalism" in *Discontinuities: New Essays on Renaissance Literature and Criticism*, edited by Viviana Comensoli and Paul Stevens and published by the University of Toronto Press, in 1998; as "Class Matters: Symbolic Boundaries and Cultural Exclusion" in *This Fine Place So Far From Home: Voices of Academics from the Working Class*, edited by C. L. Barney Dews and Carolyn Leste Law and published by Temple University Press, in 1995; and as "Still No Respect: Capitalism and the Cultural Choices of the Working Class," in *symplokē* 2.2 (1994): 159–76. My thanks to all of the editors for publishing these essays.

I am quite grateful to acknowledge a small group of friends and colleagues whose support and conversation have been more important to me than they know: at the University of Michigan Press, my editor, LeAnn Fields, whose commitment to this project ensures that it will find an audience; at Alabama, Celia Daileader, Sandy Huss, Peter Logan, Elizabeth Meese, Richard Rand, Gary Taylor, and Harold Weber; and, outside the Deep South of the United States, Alan Armstrong, Susan Bennett, Michael Bristol, Mary Cappello, Kathleen McLuskie, Jerald Spotswood, Victoria Sturtevant, Martha Woodmansee, and Janet Zandy. Two people, in particular, deserve my love and thanks: Jack Cadeaux, who challenges me to be more careful in argument, and Carol Pierman, who challenges me to be a better writer and, more importantly, a better person.

Contents

CHAPTER ONE

Introduction
Bottom Lines

W illiam Shakespeare was an upstart. In 1592, in the first surviving notice of Shakespeare as a playwright, Robert Greene warned his friends—"those Gentlemen . . . that spend their wits in making Plaies"—about the perfidious ways of actors, of

> those Puppits (I meane) that speake from our mouths, those Anticks gar-nisht in our colours. . . . Yes trust them not: for there is an upstart Crow, beautified with our feathers, that with his *Tygers heart wrapt in a Players hide, supposes he is as well able to bumbast out a blanke verse as the best of you: and being an absolute Iohannes fac totum,* is in his owne conceit the onely Shake-scene in a countrie. O that I might intreate your rare wits to be imployed in more profitable courses: & let those Apes imitate your past excellence, and never more acquaint them with your admired inventions. I know the best husband of you all will never prove an Usurer, and the kind-est of them / all will never proove a kinde nurse: yet whilst you may, seeke you better Maiotere; for it is pittie men of such rare wits, should be subject to the pleasures of such rude groomes. (Greenblatt et al. 3321–22)

As with much that concerns Shakespeare, scholars have speculated at length about the meanings of Greene's words, the exact nature of which is not known. But whether Greene thinks Shakespeare an uneducated plagiarist or an ambi-tious egotist or a vicious exploiter of the labor of others, it is clear that the dying writer believes Shakespeare to be unworthy of his success and of his ability to associate with men like himself, a gentleman educated at Cambridge.

To us, Greene's public attack and Henry Chettle's equally public apology are more astonishing than either was to Elizabethans,[1] since William Shake-speare was not then the Bard of Avon, a cultural hero, whose works ground the literary canon in English. In the 1960s, A. L. Rowse described this first surviv-

1

ing reference to Shakespeare-the-writer as a "time-bomb which has gone on reverberating ever since" (97). Even in these less Bardolatrous times, critics continue to recognize the charge contained in Greene's attack, calling it "a dig" or, more aggressively, "a slam" against the aspiring playwright (McDonald 15; B. Smith 4). Yet what interests me about this slam is a point commentators often note but seldom develop: Shakespeare *was* an upstart. Not a poet, not a man of the universities or of the court, and above all not a gentleman, Shakespeare was an actor who made his living outside the bounds of respectable and even licensed society: "masterless artificers, petty chapmen, vagabonds, sailors, criminals, players, and Puritans—all of them marginal figures in the Tudor-Stuart landscape—found themselves crowded together in the strange, extraterritorial zone outside the walls . . . of the City" (Agnew 55).

What interests me, then, about Greene's attack is not the impugning of Shakespeare's character but rather the revelation of what we would call class bias among an intellectual elite; and also that the specifics of this bias persist among contemporary intellectual elites, including critics of Shakespeare. Today, for example, I read few literary or cultural critics who agree with the proposition that the market is a legitimate arbiter of success, and rewards the worthy; or that those without formal education are capable of making art, judgments about art, or, for that matter, judgments about public policy.

I propose to return to Shakespeare later in this chapter but before doing so, I must begin to confront the problem(s) of class, which I see as this book's principal theoretical contribution to literary and cultural study. In fact, in addition to Shakespeare, the largest topics of this book are, first, the role of education in establishing and maintaining class distinction or inequality and, second, the existence, indeed the persistence, of class bias among intellectuals—a fear of the people and their judgments. But in pointing out Robert Greene's affinity with, say, Wordsworth and Coleridge, or James and Eliot, or Forster and Woolf, or Adorno and Ransom, or Frow and Patterson, I do not wish to essentialize this characteristic of the class to which I belong, or to suggest, as Shakespeare's Claudius says of death, "This must be so." Indeed, although my thinking is structural, it is not determinist. To suggest that intellectuals are hemmed in by their subject positions or social roles, by what John Frow calls "the investments we have made in knowledge and its social relations" (131), would be to deny human agency in social construction, which I do not (cf. my "Agency"). It would be to deny that we and even others outside our profession, who look "with fresh eyes and nascent ambitions at the way things are done," can and in fact do "propose changes and thereby initiate debates about 'the purpose and meaning of the activity'" we engage in (Fish, *Correctness* 23). And therefore it would be to undermine my point in writing this book about the contemporary critical reception of Shakespeare's plays. That point, at its broadest, is that to help achieve the good society and—as I shall argue in my conclusion—to protect our own most important interests, intellectuals can and should take steps to reduce their own power by reducing the power of formal education over the lives and life chances of all people.

Thirty years of the "culture wars," and specifically of debate in higher education about canons and admissions, has shown that unlike bias against women or racial minorities, bias against the working class and the poor is structurally useful and even necessary in the academy. Like John Guillory, I conclude that class bias in the academy cannot be easily eliminated. Although I support the study of working-class literature and culture in the academy and am pleased to see literary critics joining sociologists in giving attention to this work, I am skeptical—as Guillory is—about remedies for this bias based in a self-affirming identity politics that demands representation and inclusion, which have worked well if not perfectly for women and racial minorities. Guillory is skeptical about such remedies because he thinks it impossible within the academy to invoke a "self-affirmative . . . lower-class identity" (*Capital* 13). I think Guillory is right about this, but for the wrong reason, since he equates a lower-class identity with "the experience of deprivation per se" and implies that the "abolition of want" would abolish lower-class identities (13). But as sociologists, novelists, and essayists have shown, the abolition of want does not abolish lower-class identities. Thus, I would revise Guillory as follows: in the academy as we know it, the affirmation of a lower-class identity is hardly compatible with the affirmation of an (upper) middle-class identity, which is what higher education affirms. Working-class kids who succeed in the academy or subsequently in the professions are reconstituted and normalized as (upper) middle class. In the academy, working-class identity is not merely not affirmed, but actively erased.

Criticism cannot effectively challenge its own privilege, the privilege of intellectual accomplishment, which, as I argue here, contributes significantly to class privilege in the contemporary world. To me it is hardly surprising that after thirty years of the culture wars, the profession is turning today toward matters literary. Not just the Association of Literary Scholars and Critics but Stanley Fish, Frank Lentricchia, Edward Said, and Elaine Scarry, among others, have sensed that, as K. Anthony Appiah observes, identity politics and even "theory for its own sake" have lost some of their luster: "*mirabile dictu*, there are more and more literary critics . . . who actually devote themselves to . . .

literature" (44). What we need in the profession, says Edward Said, is "a patient, scrupulous reading of texts; a detailed respect for the painstaking effort for clarity of utterance; a careful attempt, in R. P. Blackmur's memorable phrase, to bring literature to performance" (3). Thirty years of the culture wars, then, have left criticism with a dilemma: our professional, indeed our intellectual self-interest, and the fact that class difference matters to both interests, is the limit beyond which we cannot go in promoting democracy or egalitarianism in the academy and consequently in society. This dilemma should not be explained away or ignored. Yet it is one whose importance we might also work to reduce. It is possible, I think, for academics to maintain our difference from the vast majority of society—to turn toward the literary, for instance—while reducing the elitism that traditionally has grounded it, the "general assumption on the part of academics that they are a superior breed" (Fish, *Correctness* 88).

Thorstein Veblen argued a century ago that, despite the appeals "made from time to time by well-meaning and sanguine persons" to "set aside the conventional aversion to labor," the irksomeness of labor *and of those who labor* is "a cultural fact" for which there is no remedy "short of a subversion of that cultural structure on which our canons of decency rest" ("Labor" 201). I do not doubt that most intellectuals are "well-meaning and sanguine persons" whose pleas for tolerance and respect of all persons both within and without the academy have achieved the kinds of "fitful" positive results Veblen also acknowledges. It is important to respect that work. But Veblen is correct: giving respect to those who do "irksome" labor is impossible until "the cultural structure [is subverted] on which our canons of decency rest."

It will not do to admit some number of working-class students to Harvard or Princeton in an attempt to turn them into versions of ourselves. The academy—and perhaps especially its humanists and artists—protects and perpetuates the cultural structure that guarantees the irksomeness of labor and of laborers. We cannot subvert it without subverting ourselves, but this is exactly what we should do: reduce the power of formal education to determine whether people will lead good lives. This means taking two courses of action: decoupling (to some extent) education and the formation of occupational opportunity; and decoupling (again, to some extent) education and the formation of cultural capital. By doing so we would undermine some, though certainly not all, of our interests as higher educators. What we would gain, I argue, is not an egalitarian society, which is not possible, but one that is considerably less stratified and unequal than today's. And in addition, as I argue in my conclusion, we would protect what to my mind is our most important interest—the freedom to do intellectually challenging work.

Guillory hints at the importance of the former coupling when he argues that the multicultural canon "merely confirms the imaginary ego ideal of a newly constituted professional-managerial class, no longer exclusively white or male" (*Capital* 38), a fact Bruce Robbins celebrates as a victory against inequality: "from the moment when knowledge of rap music or rape statistics or the genealogy of the word 'homosexual' is measured on examinations and counts toward a degree, there has been some change, . . . in access to credentials" ("Politics" 373). True enough; but as many sociologists of education and work point out, a point I develop in chapter 2, educational credentials are at the heart of inequality in contemporary societies: "in capitalist societies, the . . . tendency toward equalization of educational opportunities has been accompanied by *greater, not lesser* inequality of income distribution" (Larson, "Power" 43). What Robbins celebrates—getting "one's own experience reclassified as part of cultural capital" ("Politics" 373) or making knowledge of rap or disco music a predictor for success in law school—is, as Randall Collins argues, "an elitist reform that will have little effect on the economic prospects of the majority of women" or minorities, or working-class people generally (*Credential* 201).

Guillory implicitly recognizes the necessity of the latter coupling, arguing that we need to "disarticulate the formation of cultural capital from the class structure and the markets" (*Capital* 337). Guillory operates from the admirable premise that "*everyone* has a right of access to cultural works, to the means of both their production and their consumption" (*Capital* 54). For Guillory, such disarticulation would require us to socialize "the means of [literary] production and consumption," which in turn would require us to change the way students are evaluated in educational institutions that distribute cultural capital unequally "by governing access to the means of literary production as well as to the means of consumption (the knowledge required to read historical works)" (*Capital* 340). The weakness of this proposal for reform has been noted by a number of reviewers, and frankly, such a judgment is implicit in Guillory's own characterization of it as "only a thought experiment" (*Capital* 340). Most striking is the appearance of this plea for democracy or equality of access to higher education in a work whose rigor and style, as Robbins points out, "makes no pretense of user-friendliness beyond the academy" ("Politics" 370). Given the professionalized nature of Guillory's discourse, its opacity, we may fairly judge, as Bill Readings does, that we are "entitled to a more pointed reflection on the politics of access" (324). My guess is that Guillory does not give us this reflection because he knows it would take him where he does not want to go, which is to acknowledge that very few people have the will or the talents to do the kind of reading—or writing—he thinks everyone is or should be able to do. And acknowledging that fact might lead to another insight: to decouple the class structure and the formation of cultural capital, it is necessary, as I argue here, to decouple its formation and the educational system.

That is to say, people already have access to the means of cultural and even literary production and consumption and are producing and consuming culture and literature all the time. The problem is that what they produce and consume is devalued by institutions of education and of higher education in particular, as part of the process of creating cultural capital or a hierarchy of taste, as I argue in chapter 4. Rather than socialized education, which even Guillory admits is utopian, what we need and can achieve is more cultural democracy. Not necessarily antiliterary, cultural democracy would require only a definition of the aesthetic or the literary that is broader than the definition rooted in disinterest, which has grounded our work for almost two centuries (Woodmansee; Levine; Tompkins). Literature is not timeless or fixed, and to undermine what Martha Woodmansee calls "the interests in disinterestedness" is not to undermine the literary (11).

Guillory's failure is not just that he proposes a utopian solution to a difficult and important problem. More significantly, he proposes a solution that, if enacted even on a nonutopian scale, would enhance rather than reduce the power of educational achievement over peoples' lives. He proposes a solution that is professionally self-interested, not only in that enabling everyone to read Virgil or Machiavelli or Mill would require an enormous capital investment in education but also since more education would reduce friction between the working class and intellectuals. For it is the case, as sociologists have long pointed out, that the best predictor of liberalism on social and cultural issues is number of years of schooling. Today, the highly educated are "explicitly schooled in the culture of tolerance and pluralism" (Brint 98), but almost fifty years ago David Riesman and Nathan Glazer recognized in intellectuals' defense of civil liberties an issue that would not appeal to "the uneducated masses," for the "practice of deference and restraint . . . is understood and appreciated only among the well-to-do and highly educated strata" (78; Brint 86–87, 97–103; Croteau 195–96). Thus, as I conclude in chapter 5, it is not surprising that "more education" is promoted repeatedly by left or liberal intellectuals and politicians as an appropriate solution to both unemployment and underemployment, the part-time and contingent work that since deindustrialization has become normalized.

To consider that education might be decoupled effectively from both the formation of cultural capital and the formation of occupational opportunity is to recognize that the "social relations" implicit in the acquisition of knowledge are not everywhere the same. The uses of education in France, described by Pierre Bourdieu in *Distinction,* translate well but not exactly in North America. In the United States, the uses of education today are vastly different from what they were at the turn of the nineteenth century. In sixteenth-century England, the humanism that supplanted scholasticism served interests and privileged talents different from those that had been served and privileged before. The humanist school "neither signified an already-existing class system nor simply reproduced it; it helped reform both the ruling and the subaltern classes along the lines of a proto-bourgeois model" (Halpern, *Poetics* 26). Five years before Richard Halpern's analysis, Anthony Grafton and Lisa Jardine offered only a slightly different reading of this development, suggesting that

> the older system had fitted perfectly the needs of the Europe of the high middle ages, with its communes, its church offices open to the low-born of high talents and its vigorous debates on power and authority in state and church. The new system, we would argue, fitted the needs of the new Europe that was taking shape, with its closed governing elites, hereditary offices and strenuous efforts to close off debate on vital political and social questions. It stamped the more prominent members of the new elite with an indelible cultural seal of superiority, it equipped lesser members with fluency and the learned habit of attention to textual detail and it offered everyone a model of true culture as something given, absolute, to be mastered, not questioned—and thus fostered in all its initiates a properly docile attitude towards authority. (xiii–xiv)

One could multiply examples and appeals to authority, and span the history of education in doing so, but suffice it to say that education serves and education privileges, but different kinds of education serve and privilege differently. Without doubt, structure matters, but so does policy.

It is not controversial to say that in the United States, the most important developments in education since 1960 have been efforts to serve and privilege new kinds of students. As Richard Ohmann observes, a point to which I return in chapter 5, the state and its many agencies, including education, became in the 1960s the "arena of struggle over entitlements" as "blacks, women, Latinos, etc." were fixed as "social categories . . . by whose fortunes the legitimacy of the social order would in part be measured" ("PC" 15). The intervening years have shown that subordinate groups like women and blacks who mobilized politically and gained recognition as such official social categories—as, in the terms of this book, status groups—were able to gain increased access not just to community colleges but also to elite colleges and universities, where power and opportunity lie. At the same time, subordinate groups—like the working class—who did not mobilize politically and who were not "recognized as official social categories" did not gain similar access to elite institutions but remained pooled in institutions at the bottom of the hierarchy of higher education (Karen 210; Jacoby).

What the intervening years also have shown is that necessary to both subordinate groups' successful mobilization and their successful recognition is a *receptiveness* to their claims among privileged groups, as no doubt female and African-American activists would agree. Since the 1960s, receptiveness to the claims of women and racial minorities has been strong in higher education, and within the professional association to which I and most literary critics belong, the Modern Language Association of America. Receptiveness to the claims of the working class has been correspondingly weak, a fact made clear for literary critics in 1993 when Guillory published *Cultural Capital.* In June of that year, Janet Zandy, of the Rochester Institute of Technology, also discovered the weakness of the MLA's receptiveness to the claims of class. Zandy was informed by the director of convention programs for the MLA, Maribeth T. Kraus, that her proposal to establish a permanent MLA discussion group on working-class literature, a proposal supported by 160 members of the association, had been rejected by the Program Committee and the MLA executive council. Currently active discussion groups in the MLA include groups on Arthurian literature, on Sephardic studies, and on the two-year college; 1997 saw the addition of a discussion group on disability studies. And yet Kraus informed Zandy that the proposal was rejected because it did not offer a definition of class that could clearly identify a set of working-class literary texts (Kraus).

The MLA blames Zandy; her proposal did not define the concept of class so as to easily identify working-class literature. Having seen Zandy's proposal, I cannot help but suspect some disingenuousness in the MLA's criticism of it: one could make the same criticism about Karl Marx who, it is now clear, did not adequately define class so as to easily identify the flow of history. In the case of studying working-class literature within the institutional context of the MLA, moreover, the burden of definitional proof would seem to be low: working-class literature is literature by or for—or even about—members of the working class. The definition of working class would seem to be little more difficult than the definition of any other kind of literature to be addressed by MLA discussion groups—Canadian, Celtic, Hebrew, Jewish-American, Slavic, and so on. Such definitions are working definitions, and questions arise continuously about whether a given author or work "fits" into a given category of literature.

This is not to say, however, that literary critics can or should dispense with an attempt to define the concept, or to understand its history, a point to which I turn next. Before doing so, I must claim that the MLA's response to Zandy's proposal reveals more than just unreceptiveness to the claims of class: the unreceptiveness itself is rooted in a class bias that is inherent in the professional study of literature, as well as in higher education more generally.

Part—but only part—of the reason why class is often invoked but rarely invoked seriously is that, as the MLA observes, the concept is difficult both to define and to apply. Complex and difficult debate about how to define class has existed since the nineteenth century, and no one—not Marx or Max Weber early on, or Erik Olin Wright or Pierre Bourdieu today—can claim to have gotten it right. Yet precisely because class is not, say, the second law of thermodynamics, those of us attempting to cross disciplinary boundaries to discuss the relationships of "class" to literature and literary production, should, I think, grapple with at least the principal points of debate in sociology: is class determined by one's role in capitalist production? Or is class determined as well— or perhaps even more so—by educational or cultural achievements? Is class a measure for potential conflict in society? Or is class rather a way to describe a social hierarchy? How is class reproduced? Are there only two classes? Or three? Or four? Does class matter? Answers to these questions will vary, and no set of answers will satisfy everyone, but to answer the questions means entering the debate. It means coming to terms with the legacies of both Karl Marx and Max Weber, a task sociologists have struggled with since before the turn of the last century.

Since a precise definition of class is unwieldy, likely to be outmoded—or disputed—tomorrow, I wish in discussing class to follow Guillory's lead and to "construct . . . the concept through the contexts of its deployment" (*Capital* 341 n. 1). Nevertheless, it is clear that the concept is useful to the extent that it explains, or helps to explain, inequality or stratification; and that in this regard, the problem confounding most theorists is the relationship between economic and cultural determinants of class. A corollary problem is to identify the class position of intellectuals. Regarding the former, Guillory has recognized the need to bring together Marx and Weber and, as I do here, concludes that "the most obvious way to resolve such a theoretical tension would be to redefine class in such a way that it assumes both economic and cultural constituents" ("Intellectuals" 124). Other writers offer different solutions. For example, accepting the Marxian notion that two classes exist in conflict, Alvin W. Gouldner sees the possessors of cultural capital, whom he calls the New Class, as the historical *successor* to the propertied bourgeoisie (20–21). Frow, in contrast, acknowledges the burgeoning power of the New Class but continues to insist "that there are other and more decisive powers" than knowledge (120), specifically, "ownership of the means of production" (125). James Livingston disagrees with both, suggesting contra Frow that corporate capitalism and consumer culture have moved us "beyond the proprietary stage of capitalism" and thus "beyond a society defined by relations of production" (85, 118). But, contra Gouldner, Livingston does not redefine class in terms of the possession of cultural capital; in Livingston's view, as the emphasis in economics shifts from production to consumption, "class gives way . . . to alternative principles of social organization such as race and gender" (78). For Livingston, class must "recede" in importance as a principle of social organization in a society where "consumption and its connotations . . . matter more than production and its requirements" (78, 77).

What is peculiar in Livingston's analysis, especially given its focus on the late nineteenth century, is the absence of Weber: Weber called status groups what Livingston calls "alternative principles of social organization" rooted in "consumption and its connotations." As I explain in chapter 3, Weber describes stratification by status as the distribution of prestige in a society; and a claim of social prestige is based primarily in "a specific *style of life*" (932, 927, and passim). For Weber, the contrast between a class and a status group is, among other things, the difference between "production and consumption. Whereas class expresses relationships involved in production, status groups express those involved in consumption, in the form of specific 'styles of life'" (Giddens 43–44).

Status groups antedate classes, and Livingston is correct to suggest that "class was determined by the development of capitalism" (78). But the development of classes never eliminated the power of status groups; and the development of consumer culture will not eliminate the power of class.[2] As Anthony Giddens explains, "the point of Weber's analysis is not that class and status constitute two 'dimensions of stratification', but that classes and status communities represent two possible, and competing, modes of group formation in relation to the distribution of power in society" (44). This distinction Guillory acknowledges as well: in the academy's culture wars, the "equation of gender, race, and class as commensurable minority identities effaces" precisely the structural "distinction between class and *status*" (*Capital* 13).

Livingston's argument about class works not only because he occludes the Weberian argument about status but also because he subscribes to a Marxian definition of class, one linked to production and in which there are two classes of people, the propertied and the propertyless. But Weber, who theorized class in terms of market capacities and life chances, insisted upon distinctions within the propertied class and within the propertyless. And within both, skill and education are two sorts of capital that in class terms decisively distinguish their possessors from those who possess property or worse, only their unskilled labor. Accordingly, class theories fall into the Weberian rather than into the Marxian tradition when they recognize three or more classes and base class difference not only on property but on education and skill.

Indeed, the current "crisis" about whether class is a useful concept for literary analysis arguably results from critics' failure to attend seriously to theoretical and empirical work on class and stratification outside the Marxian tradition. This theoretical narrowness results in the failure to distinguish class from status, such that, as I argue in chapter 3, the two terms become synonyms in many cases, allowing for slippage and imprecision in describing the workings of inequality and difference. In addition, the focus on Marxian theory disables frank assessment of the middle class and, in particular, of the New Class of intellectuals. Confusion results especially, I think, from the fact that education and its institutions and practitioners affect both class hierarchies and status hierarchies. That is, class is associated with production and thus with markets, and status is associated with consumption and thus with cultural groups; but education—and higher education in particular—affects the construction of both in complicated ways. Education affects production, for example, through the implementation of scientific management or technical expertise; it affects consumption through the implementation of taste. Whether cultural capital is a historical successor to financial capital or just another kind of capital, and whether the class hierarchy is separate from or overlaps with or doubles the status hierarchy[3]—all these are empirical questions that remain open. But it is clear that in modern market societies, education is doubly oppressive to the vast majority of people, making their jobs worse—flipping burgers—and judging as poor their choices as consumers—eating what they flip.

Wai-Chee Dimock and Michael T. Gilmore explain their attempt to rethink class for literary studies as just such a response to "the imminent demise of Marxism, evidenced by the collapse of the Soviet Union and Eurocommunism," a demise that

> would seem to mark the demise as well of "class" as a category of analysis. How can we continue to use the word with any sense of political efficacy,

when its instrumental expression—"class struggle"—has ceased to be a vital historical force? And how can we continue to use the word with any sense of analytic authority, when the privileged subject of that analysis— the "working class"—has thus far shown no sign of being a privileged locus of agency, so that the vocabulary of class has come to seem no more than a flat description, a matter of taxonomy, shorn of the animating coloration of will and necessity, incipience and dialectic? (1)

The Marxian coloration of this is surely obvious. Dimock and Gilmore indicate that for most literary critics "class" had stable meanings until very recently, meanings entirely bound up with Marxism and now shaken by Marxism's failures. Unfamiliar with, and in some cases contemptuous of debate in sociology and economics, many critics seem to have gotten the causal relationship backward: as if "class" came into being with Marx, rather than, arguably, the other way around. Marx offered an alternative to interpretations of class and capital posited by the classical political economists, but he was not the only thinker to do so, and literary critics have largely ignored what many though not all Marxists dismissively refer to as bourgeois sociology, the tradition of analysis I have been discussing, with roots in the work of Weber and Durkheim, among others. If the collapse of the Soviet Union unsettles the hegemony of Marxian understandings of class within literary criticism, allowing us to see class as "itself an analyzable artifact . . . to be scrutinized, contextualized, critiqued for its commissions and omissions" (Dimock and Gilmore 2), this is all very much to the good. It is also a richly ironic example of superstructure following base.

Equally obvious in Dimock and Gilmore's lines is an attempt to represent—if I may indulge such a notion—the communal or general mind of the profession, a profession that is hugely disappointed by the working class, which "failed in its historical mission of emancipation" (Laclau and Mouffe 169). As I shall suggest in the chapters to follow, particularly chapters 2 and 5, working-class kids know very well what are the consequences of disappointing your teachers by failing to subscribe to or internalize the norms of (upper) middle-class culture: punishment and, ultimately, reassignment to the working class. Normally, of course, working-class kids don't fail History; they fail courses in history, or they fail to subscribe to the rules of grammar, or they fail to attend in class to anything the teacher says. But for the working class as a whole, the consequences of failing History are quite similar to the consequences of an individual working-class kid's failing a course in history: Is it coincidence—or irony—that the exclusion since the late 1960s of the working class from left and liberal political and social agendas, including those institutionalized in the

Democratic Party (or the MLA, for that matter), follows hard upon the working class's failure as an emancipatory force and its subsequent resistance to some parts of those agendas, including, for example, busing, welfare, immigration, affirmative action, or gay rights?

Such estrangement makes it difficult to accept at face value Robbins's criticism of Guillory for adopting a concept of class that, he claims, "allows for no active relationship between classes, no pressure from below, no hegemonic concession from above, no dynamic of articulation whereby fractions of different classes enter into and fall out of alliance with each other." Nevertheless, let's take Robbins seriously: what this means, according to Robbins, is that "unlike Marx or Gramsci," neither Guillory nor Bourdieu allows "that professionals and nonprofessionals might ever have common rather than merely local interests." Because each insists that professionals and the working class hold different interests, neither Guillory nor Bourdieu offers him a "real politics for professional academics" but only "another means of humanistic self-flagellation" ("Politics" 374).

That Robbins is disappointed to read another account of his responsibility for inequality is not surprising. Nor is it surprising that in order to avoid self-flagellation, he marshals his substantial intellectual resources to posit intellectuals and professionals as groups committed to social and economic equality. To be sure, the "politics of the alibi," as Frow calls it, "whereby intellectuals claim the right to speak from a position of relative power on behalf of the powerless and the dispossessed" (168), has a long and distinguished history among intellectuals, the current version of which, according to Nancy Armstrong and Leonard Tennenhouse, begins with Marx himself, who protected his theory of capital by concealing the plain fact that in "modern cultures the people in charge are always literate people who determine what literacy is, how one acquires it, and therefore who has access to the specific knowledge and privileges accompanying it (138). Or as Bourdieu puts it, making the same point rather more broadly, "the celebrated 'universal class,' be it Hegel's Prussian bureaucracy or Marx's proletariat, was never more than a straw-man for intellectuals who designated themselves as the ultimate judges of universality in their designation of the 'universal class'" ("Corporatism" 109).

Like Weber, writers such as Bourdieu, Gouldner, Guillory, or Armstrong and Tennenhouse shift the locus of power from capital toward cultural capital, toward intellect. And if, as Robbins complains, such writers insist on seeing the classes formed thereby as holding largely incompatible interests, it is arguable that in doing so and regardless of whether they subscribe to a two-class model of stratification, these writers nevertheless remain to some extent within the

Marxian tradition. For certainly it is the case, as Ralf Dahrendorf explained decades ago, that

> however one may interpret, extend, or improve Marx, classes in his sense are clearly not layers in a hierarchical system of strata differentiated by gradual distinctions. . . . *Class* is always a category for purposes of the analysis of the dynamics of social conflict and its structural roots. (76)

For Marx, class is an analytic concept useful in understanding social conflict and the possibilities for organized action by a group. A class, according to Peter Berger, has "vested interests in common, interests that must always be pursued *against* other interests" (52).

Several recent writers—Bourdieu in "The Corporatism of the Universal," Frow in *Cultural Studies and Cultural Value,* and Guillory in "Literary Critics as Intellectuals"—acknowledge this point, an acknowledgment enhanced, in my view, by each writer's equally strong recognition that political conflicts and divisions are to be found within this class of intellectuals (that is, within the New Class, as Gouldner put it, or the professional-managerial class, as Barbara and John Ehrenreich put it). Empirical research suggests that "far from becoming filled with 'tenured radicals,' the professoriat has included an increasing number of self-described conservatives in the 1980s and a declining proportion of liberals," *especially* on economic issues, issues about which, like others in the upper middle class, we continue to offer opinions significantly more conservative than those offered by the working class (Brint 154, 86–87, 97–103; Croteau 195–96). Further, the 1980s have made it clear that such divisions exist not only between, say, economists and philosophers but also between literary critics, with Allan Bloom criticized by his peers as roundly as if he were Ronald Reagan. That conservative political positions are held by literary critics as well as by engineers undermines the construction of the intellectual "as innately progressive, always potentially subversive" and furthermore reveals the "covert elitism" such a construction entails (Guillory, "Intellectuals" 111, 121).

This "covert elitism" is easy to detect: the claim of autonomy, a class interest usually described more grandly as the ability to speak truth to power, allows certain intellectuals to claim that their political judgments are similarly autonomous—objective and disinterested and therefore superior to the judgments of other, interested parties. Frow, for example, invokes a class interest to promote political desire: "there are clear limits to the extent to which it is possible for intellectuals to associate themselves with anti-intellectualism; and there are limits to how far they can or should suspend their critique of, for example, racism, sexism, and militarism" (158). The effect—and perhaps the intent—of this sequence is to link intellectualism with "the critique of . . . racism, sexism, and militarism," thus requiring assent for the latter to follow naturally upon assent for the former. Needless to say, many intellectuals will resist the flow of Frow's rhetoric, without sacrificing their intellectuality, or even their opposition to sexism or racism, a point Guillory or Steven Brint might make as well.

Given that, as Frow himself makes clear, there is no escape from interested-ness, it is arguable that intellectuals should distinguish even more carefully between class interests and political desire, between, for example, an autonomy that is essential to our work and an end to sexism in, say, the Catholic Church that is not. For ourselves as intellectuals, such focusing can only be beneficial: cloaking a political agenda behind a supposed disinterestedness ultimately dis-credits both the agenda and our actual interests. Furthermore, that intellectu-als and the working class hold different and sometimes opposing interests in both economic and social policy, and that occasionally they do battle over those interests, does not disable a "real politics for professional academics," as Robbins claims. Indeed, conflict over interests is perhaps a stronger condition for such a politics than are common interests. Common interests offer intellec-tuals and workers the opportunity to work as a coalition, which in practice means that intellectuals dominate the proceedings and give up nothing. As Frow concedes, when confronted by a disagreeable set of criteria for judgment, the standard maneuver of those vested in high culture and its institutions has been to impose their own, more agreeable set of criteria, precisely because they "have . . . the power to do so" (151). Conflict over interests offers the opportu-nity for intellectuals to compromise, the opportunity for us to give and take rather than merely dictate.

As promised and to help conclude this chapter, let me return briefly to Shake-speare; that is, forward to the past. Toward the end of *A Midsummer Night's Dream*, Theseus, Duke of Athens, wonders how his court shall "wear away this long age of three hours / Between our after-supper and bed-time?" (V.i.33–34). Offered a list of ready entertainments, the Duke settles his curiosity upon "'A tedious brief scene of young Pyramus / And his love Thisbe, very tragical mirth'" (ll. 56–57), a play Philostrate, the Master of the Revels, immediately describes as indeed tedious and brief, and very tragical mirth:

A play there is, my lord, some ten words long,
Which is as brief as I have known a play;

But by ten words, my lord, it is too long,
Which makes it tedious; for in all the play
There is not one word apt, one player fitted.
And tragical, my noble lord, it is,
For Pyramus therein doth kill himself;
Which, when I saw rehears'd, I must confess
Made mine eyes water; but more merry tears
The passion of loud laughter never shed.

(ll. 61–70)

Although Philostrate's critical judgment fails to convince Theseus to choose another entertainment, his emphasis on propriety, taste, and style foreshadows the responses to the play that will be offered by the assembled audience of Theseus's court: both play and players, the aristocrats tell us, are ungoverned, disordered, uncouth, childlike, and error-ridden (ll. 123, 125, 353, 122, 237). *Pyramus and Thisbe* is the work of "hard-handed men . . . / Which never labour'd in their minds till now," and it is, as Hippolyta concludes, "the silliest stuff that ever I heard" (ll. 72–73, 207).

Louis Montrose is correct to conclude that at the turn of the seventeenth century, the "ideological positioning" of *A Midsummer Night's Dream* and of its play-within-the-play "is more complex and more equivocal than can be accommodated by the terms of an elite/popular opposition" (*Playing* 198). On the one hand, *Dream* mocks or burlesques the efforts of the amateur thespians. This mockery is part of a strategy of professionalization, by which Shakespeare distinguishes "the mechanicals' art from that of the Lord Chamberlain's Men." At the same time, such professionalization itself is encouraged by the Elizabethan regime as part of its strategy to suppress "performances of the civic Corpus Christi plays and . . . other forms of popular pastime" (*Playing* 196, 182). On the other hand, *Dream*'s mockery of Bottom, Quince, Snug, and the rest of the amateur players works to parody the professional actors' own "relationship to their patrons and to the state" and thus to distance the professional theater from "the pressures and constraints of aristocratic and royal patronage" (*Playing* 196, 205).

Yet even if "Shakespeare is no more clearly aristocratic in his biases here than he is plebian" (Montrose *Playing* 196), the oppositions invoked by the aristocrats in response to the mechanicals' work—mind/body, order/disorder, adult/child, governed/ungoverned, and refined/uncouth, to which we might add elite/popular—have displayed remarkable staying power and serve nicely to characterize elite assumptions about "rude mechanicals" even in late-twentieth-century America, as I hope the following chapters will demonstrate. Not timeless or universal, these binaries yet seem to be necessary to how elites construct themselves and their power, whether the elite is composed of aristocrats who insist upon traditional prerogatives based on blood and title or of professionals who insist upon prerogatives based on achieved intellectual expertise or ethical disinterest.

In 1934, John Dewey observed: "Auguste Comte said that the great problem of our time is the organization of the proletariat into the social system" (344). And then he added: "the remark is even truer now than when it was made." My sense is that the remark remains at least as true today. Certainly it is the case, as Guillory convincingly argues, that within the academy, and "within the discourse of liberal pluralism" more generally, the invocation of class, of the proletariat, as part of a multicultural holy trinity is an "empty" gesture (*Capital* 14). In writing this book, I have attempted to understand why this is so, and why the intellectual culture that trained me and in which I now work training others, an intellectual culture that nowadays values diversity and pluralism above almost all other virtues, despises people like the working-class people I grew up with. Such a desire is not simply personal or local, although my personal history informs each of these essays and sometimes emerges in them as anecdote or story, in characteristic postmodern fashion (cf. Simpson). Rather and more importantly, it is a desire to understand what passes for truth in literary study today, why some questions are asked and answered, and others are not.

Like this chapter, each of the chapters to follow originates in an interrogation that puts social class at the center of the analysis, and not just the issue of class in Shakespeare's plays or in early modern England, but the issue of class in the academy and in this society today. Shakespeare has indeed hit the "big time" in contemporary culture, and as Michael Bristol argues, in the United States "every expression of interest in Shakespeare, both amateur and professional, is . . . an unambiguous sign of cultural advancement" (*Big* 3; *America* 1). To get at the meanings of this sign, and thereby to contribute to a needed reexamination of class as an analytic concept in literary and cultural study, I bring together a range of theoretical and empirical work on class, some of it unfamiliar to literary critics. This work also allows me to enter an ongoing debate about the politics of academic literary study and of the academy more generally, and I offer here a point of view that builds upon even as it challenges work on this topic by John Guillory, Evan Watkins, John Frow, Bruce Robbins, and Stanley Fish. For these reasons—and not just because Shakespeare remains central to literary and cultural work in English—I hope to find readers whose specialties are not necessarily Shakespeare or early modern English literature or indeed who are not academics at all.[4] I search here for a usable past, one that helps all of us to envision and achieve a better future.

Beginning in the early modern period and continuing to this day, three institutions principally offer individuals the opportunity to improve, via success, or worsen, via failure, their lots in life: educational institutions, economic institutions, and political institutions.[5] I propose to assess some of the ways these institutions manage inequality by reading each through a Shakespearean text: in chapter 2, pairing educational institutions with *The Tempest;* in chapter 3, pairing economic institutions with *Timon of Athens;* and, in chapter 4, pairing political institutions with *Coriolanus.* I propose that these institutions manage inequality variously, and that each privileges or devalues certain kinds of behavior and hence privileges or devalues certain kinds of persons. These institutions, therefore, produce interested parties, and to the extent that these interests are incompatible, so too are not only the institutions but also their aficionados and loyalists. Obviously, since all of these institutions produce all of us, divided loyalties can and will exist and persist within individuals. Still, some of us define ourselves in terms of one institution more than another, and therefore some of us may align ourselves rather more exclusively with the values and interests of that institution. Thus, in chapter 5, I offer an example of the strengths of such loyalties today and focus—via a discussion of the pastoral and enclosure—on the politics of contemporary land-use, of leisure and environmentalism, in Ashland, Oregon, the home of the Oregon Shakespeare Festival. And in my conclusion I attempt to place this book's arguments within a larger debate about loyalties, one that has erupted recently between what have been called the "social" Left and the "cultural" Left, and that extends to the nature of professional life in the university.

I am interested in how these institutions appear not just to intellectuals but also to working-class people. Looked at from both perspectives, it is clear why intellectuals and working-class people find themselves at loggerheads: intellectuals consistently promote political and educational institutions as ways to solve society's ills, and workers perceive political and educational institutions as potentially hostile to their interests and needs. Since the end of World War II, intellectuals have proposed cultural solutions—diversity, tolerance—to social problems, and workers have proposed, or at least wanted, economic solutions—higher wages, lower taxes, a more favorable distribution of wealth. I do not deny the history of radical thought and activity among the working class; nor do I deny the potential importance of both education and government in securing workers' interests. But generally speaking, workers see that the solution to their problems is a job with a decent wage and the opportunity to purchase goods at a decent price.

It was largely for this reason that Lenin theorized and implemented the leadership of an intellectual vanguard: workers do not see the need for revolution because their interests are addressed very well by the efforts of trade unionism (May 21). According to Gouldner, Lenin understood that "socialism could not be spontaneously created by the proletariat" precisely because Marxism was not their movement: "Marxism was the creation of educated intellectuals" and reflected their consciousness, not that of workers or peasants. After all, Gouldner aptly reminds us, "Marxism itself was made . . . by the son of a minor Prussian bureaucrat and the son of a multi-national industrialist, both of mandarin culture" (76–77).

Workers favor markets and capitalism because, as I will argue in chapters 3 and 4, these institutions promote "a widening of opportunity rather than the maintenance of privileges" (Tawney, *Usury* 135). Intellectuals favor education and politics because we must insist, finally, on the maintenance of privileges. For us, as Frow contends, "there is no escape from the consequences of possession of cultural capital, just as there is no way of getting outside the game of value judgement and the game of cultural distinction" (168–69). Some of us may try to do so, and some of us may be perfectly correct in our attitudes toward the working class: more concerned with the negative effects of NAFTA on jobs than with its positive effects on our TIAA-CREF accounts—and willing to sacrifice the latter; able to accept that Reagan Democrats had legitimate reasons for abandoning the Democratic Party—and willing to change the policies that led to their leaving; and convinced, with Herbert J. Gans, that when it comes to culture, "every one is entitled to choose what he or she considers good" ("Popular" 20), even when those choices include professional wrestling, representational art, and the clothes sold at Wal-Mart.

Some of us may even act on our attitudes and in ways more significant than just voting, by giving time and money to various political causes, for example. Nevertheless, along with Brint and Fish, I think it important to distinguish between the political effects of our various social roles. Fish states flatly that "academic work is one thing and political work another" (*Correctness* 93), but Brint develops the distinction, suggesting that "the institutions staffed by liberal professionals may have one sort of political import, while the people who make them up, in their activity as private citizens, may have quite another" (97). Such a "contradiction" between the personal and the professional is perfectly normal, and many of my friends and colleagues live with it daily, but just as many, if not more, do not seem content to do so. Robbins, for example, wants oppositionality to be constitutive not just of his self but of his professional role as well: he wants to be an agent of critique from inside the gates of the institution (*Vocations* 55).

My difficulty with this desire is partly semantic: what does oppositionality or critique mean in this instance? Here I would echo Fish, who insists that as long as we labor within the gates, "the changes we might make will be in the nature of modifications rather than ruptures" (*Correctness* 101). Modifications not ruptures, or perhaps we might say, reform not revolution. If this is in fact the case, then the question is whether for Robbins oppositionality or critique means reform and modification or revolution and rupture. If the latter, then such oppositionality is impossible, doomed to failure, as Fish persuasively argues. If the former, then oppositionality or critique is not very oppositional, and while puffing up reform in such a manner may fool other academics or intellectuals, it does not fool workers or other marginalized folks who recognize such moves as typical: workers know, says Raymond Williams, that our "one identifiable activity seems to be using words or statistics to confuse or screw you" (*Hope* 144).

Still, let us grant Robbins the possibility or even the actuality that, in Nancy Fraser's words, "the radical academic is not an oxymoron" (cited by Robbins, *Vocations* 55). The problem remains that such people are and always have been a minority. As Williams points out, "most intellectuals, even now after changes in education, either come from or soon identify with the ruling or privileged classes" (*Hope* 144). Despite their expansion, educational institutions are "still deeply distorted by the effects of class and privilege" (*Hope* 145), and they remain distorted for reasons having to do with their structure, as I argue in chapter 2: "bringing new grist to your mill does not in itself alter the basic manner of its operation" (Fish, *Correctness* 101). And therefore, concludes Williams, who speaks *"from the inside, from my own real world,"* the fact of the matter is that workers and "the labour movement *[do] not distrust intellectuals and educators nearly enough"* (*Hope* 145; emphasis added).

Williams himself is exemplary, an intellectual of great wisdom and courage, bred in the working class. And for many of today's left intellectuals "he will remain . . . an alibi," as one of the anonymous readers of this manuscript suggests. That my reader is correct, I have little doubt, but I dare say Williams himself would be horrified—might even, perhaps, turn in his grave—to learn that part of his legacy is to provide an alibi for intellectuals who *need* to believe, with Robbins, "that what we do is meaningful," that "oppositional work" is conceivable within the professions, and thus that the "professions are not, in Shaw's phrase, conspiracies against the laity" (*Vocations* x, 91).

Robbins admits that what he does in *Secular Vocations* includes "an element of personal apologia" because "when lower-middle-class values join with an elite education to produce some form of academic leftism, as they have for me and many others . . . the embarrassments of possessing expertise in a deeply unjust society cannot be wished away" (x). My work here is not an apologia but rather an expression of guilt, perhaps even of survivor's guilt, and it, too, cannot be wished away. My guilt carries with it not embarrassment, which disappeared years ago when I left my hard-hat, blue-collar neighborhood, but rather a complex mixture of anger, shame, and pride. This book, however, is not memoir; it does not recount nor does it depend upon "the personal history that brought [me] into this arena of evidence" (Fish, *Correctness* 95). Rather and *pace* Fish's defense of the protocols of literary professionalism, this book is the result of many years of thinking, which has been disciplined—perhaps not enough by the norms of my profession (*Correctness* 94–95, 47–48). I believe my conclusions to be true, but I do not expect my readers to agree with all I say here, and I know it is not for me to decide whether Robbins's conclusions or mine (or Fish's or Guillory's) are closer to the truth, closer to being correct about whether (literary) professionalism today is or is not a kind of conspiracy against the laity. But I offer here for your consideration a case that, for better or worse, it is.

CHAPTER TWO

"Burn but his books"
Intellectual Domination in *The Tempest*

"*I* believe this community is a hard-hat community and very few hard hats take in Shakespeare. They're more *Oklahoma* types. I'd like to see [the company do] more things that the citizens of Garden Grove would come out to." So reasoned City Councilman Raymond T. Littrell, as he and other members of the council in my hometown of Garden Grove, California, decided in June 1988 to withdraw an eighty-three-thousand-dollar subsidy from the Grove Shakespeare Festival (Herman). An interesting argument, this: for while city councils sometimes debate the value of subsidizing arts organizations, a debate often conducted over cultural taste, the relative merits of *West Side Story* and *Romeo and Juliet,* seldom do the naysayers imply that the subsidy might be justified if the arts organization produced dinner as well as theater.

For five years, the Grove Shakespeare Festival limped along, each year securing funding from various sources to make up the shortfall and to contribute to Orange County's cultural life. Shakespeare is hard to shake, even in a city almost adjacent to Disneyland whose principal claim to fame is, locally, its part in a burgeoning Little Saigon and, nationally, its status as the headquarters for a successful television preacher. Often, though, as I read and think and write about Shakespeare or the canon or literary theory, the fuss over the Grove Shakespeare Festival comes to mind. When it does, I know that what bothers me about the councilman's remarks is not that they almost deny the very possibility of me, the daughter of a hard hat who grew up in Garden Grove and became a Shakespearean, nor even that they homogenize and stereotype the working-class constituents the councilman is elected to represent. I realize instead that basically the councilman is correct, and that as an academic I am strongly implicated in reasons why "very few hard hats take in Shakespeare."

To understand why few hard hats take in Shakespeare requires one to confront the role intellectuals play in the creation and reproduction of class distinction, of inequality. Facing such hard truths about academic work and its functions in society is not an easy task, particularly for a literary radicalism whose "characteristic feature," according to Aijaz Ahmad, is its failure to address "the question of its own determination by the conditions of its production and the class location of its agents" (6). Yet not all literary critics have failed in the way lamented by Ahmad: John Frow, John Guillory, Bruce Robbins, and Evan Watkins have said much recently about the class location of intellectuals and about the functions of education in society. Here I would like to begin a short discussion of those functions by developing certain points alluded to in the previous chapter. As noted there, Guillory clings to the notion that socialized education "would disarticulate the formation of cultural capital from the class structure"; but at the same time he acknowledges that the university, in particular, "is not . . . a *representative* place" (*Capital* 337, 37). The university is an institution whose principal function in society is to distinguish, to separate, to launch those deemed meritorious. The privileging of intellectual work, the judging of intellectual merit, is itself a principal way in which society reproduces itself.[1]

The university is not representative because it is exclusive, the preserve of an elite, who have demonstrated their difference in the lower levels of the educational system. I am writing this book—rather than waitressing or driving a bus or cleaning up at Disneyland or being unemployed, like the kids I grew up with—in large part because in class, I demonstrated my difference from them. Willing and appropriate, that is, meritorious, material on which to work, I was classed in class, eventually to be eased or wrenched from the culture of my birth and reconstituted more or less successfully according to the norms of (upper) middle-class culture—Standard English, taste, manners—four words that must stand in here for dozens of telling behavioral differences. Richard Terdiman is correct: in class, we learn to class (227). And some of us learn that we belong no longer to the working class.

One of the aims of this book is to counteract the denial of difference implicit in the (self) identification of almost every American as middle class. In this book, therefore, I will often modify *middle class* with a parenthetical *upper* in order to indicate that interests and assumptions so labeled are different from those of the working class. In addition, I refer to my own occupational group (college and university professors) as the upper middle class, sans parentheses. Many of my readers will disagree, and some humanists in particular will insist on claiming working-class status, because "plumbers make more money than I do" or because "I belong to a union, too." Yet a glance at the professorate's salaries, published in the *Chronicle of Higher Education* (26), reveals that, on average, we fall in or very near the top quintile of incomes in the United

States—even discounting the fact that we are paid only for nine months of work.

Furthermore, and as it is also one of the aims of this book to argue, one cannot define class distinction in purely economic terms. When one defines class as including cultural capital as well as financial capital, that is, when one looks at the status hierarchy as relevant to or even doubling the class hierarchy, one cannot help but describe the professorate as upper middle class, since in both the United States and in Europe, professors hold extremely high status, similar to that accorded to physicians and federal court judges (Treiman 141–42, 318–19). Moreover, cultural capital is not just a ranking on a chart; it involves lived experience, and professors are part of a social world that is culturally different from that of the working class. Notwithstanding political divisions among professors or professionals generally, to which I alluded in chapter 1, empirical evidence suggests that as a group professionals do think of themselves as part of a "social and cultural club" (Derber, Schwartz, and Magrass 160). Debate continues about just how distinctive this club is from that of managers and executives—Derber, Schwartz, and Magrass think quite a lot (157–60), but Brint, for example, thinks not much, which in itself is a conclusion of significant political import. But it is clear, as Barbara Ehrenreich points out to Bruce Robbins, that professors of literature and, say, chemical engineers "live in the same neighborhoods, go to the same social events, marry each other, and hope that their children turn out to have similar occupations. (The professor of lit may be mildly disappointed if his or her child turns out to be an engineer, and vice versa; both, however, would be devastated if the child becomes a forklift operator). Most of what is interesting about a class derives from its *social* existence, and its hopes for reproducing itself, in castelike fashion, from one generation to the next" (Robbins, "Interview" 175).

In class, then, I learned that, if all went well, I would no longer be working class. I learned as well what every ex-working-class academic or professional learns, even if she or he will not acknowledge it: "school knowledge is loaded in class terms" (Aronowitz and Giroux 12). Historians and sociologists make clear that since their beginnings in the nineteenth century, what the schools and universities teach is, principally, (upper) middle-class Anglo-Protestant norms of behavior. Grades and other measures of ability such as intelligence tests predict success within the various levels and institutions of education—and not necessarily success on the job or in life.[2] Only to the extent, therefore, that educational success is tied to occupational opportunities does education contribute to inequality and the reproduction of inequality. Unfortunately (for those concerned about equality), in this society those bonds are very tight indeed: Randall Collins points out that "modern America has come to be stratified around an educational credential system with a stranglehold on occupational opportunities" (*Credential* 8; Bledstein; Larson, *Rise;* Derber, Schwartz, and Magrass). Even worse is that equal access to education appears not to weaken the link between education and inequality. As Magali Sarfatti Larson explains, "in capitalist societies, the postwar tendency toward equalization of educational opportunities has been accompanied by *greater, not lesser* inequality of income distribution" ("Power" 43).

Throughout the twentieth century the public school system has provided an ideological resolution to the tension between merit and equality: "mass access to the lower echelons of the public school system allows the higher levels of the educational hierarchy to claim meritocratic legitimations for their selection of entrants" and for the many social privileges eventually to be acquired by those entrants (Larson, *Rise* 136; Derber, Schwartz, and Magrass 82–91). Thus, even if, like Watkins, one does not want to dismiss "educational ideals as simply ideals—as 'false promises' or just 'wrong'—"(*Throwaways* 74), it remains the case that what principally constitutes the likelihood of social mobility or of the reproduction of the social order is not—as Guillory would have it—"access to the means of literary production and consumption" (*Capital* ix) or even the development of academic skills generally. Rather, it is a willingness to conform to and preferably to internalize the culture of the (upper) middle class, a culture that, since its emergence in the early nineteenth century, has remained remarkably consistent in its standards of sociability and propriety. Then as now, and perhaps now more than ever, (upper) middle-class culture emphasizes qualities such as "self-discipline, physical fitness, dietary control, temperance, and sexual restraint" (Bledstein 26; Derber, Schwartz, and Magrass 91–97). Indeed, nineteenth-century moralists might envy the list of contemporary (upper) middle-class prohibitions: perfume, fast food, red meat, furs and leather, guns, garish or even large signage on buildings and businesses, cigarettes, alcohol, marijuana, cocaine, LSD, unsafe sex—and no sex, remember, is entirely safe.

Perhaps not surprisingly, compliance with such an agenda is achieved most often with (upper) middle-class students, who "identify with teachers and authority figures and learn to play the system effectively to reap its rewards" (Croteau 156). Working-class students, as Paul Willis has shown in his classic ethnography, *Learning to Labor,* often actively resist this socialization (or domination) and thus (intentionally) reproduce themselves as uneducated workers, contemptible in their habits of dissipation, in persisting in doing what they know—or should know—is not in their best interests. Consider Miranda's judgment of her attempts to educate Caliban:

> I pitied thee,
> Took pains to make thee speak, taught thee each hour
> One thing or other: when thou didst not, savage,
> Know thine own meaning, but wouldst gabble like
> A thing most brutish, I endow'd thy purposes
> With words that made them known. But thy vile race,
> Though thou didst learn, had that in't which good natures
> Could not abide to be with; therefore wast thou
> Deservedly confin'd to this rock,
> Who hadst deserv'd more than a prison.
>
> (I.ii.355–65)

Caliban is intelligent enough—he learns—but he does not *behave*.

On this point, to bring together Guillory and Collins, as well as Shakespeare, is to suggest that a desire for "the means of literary production and consumption" *is* part of (upper) middle-class culture, that which is learned (or not) in school and which is essential to occupational success. It is to acknowledge, as Burton J. Bledstein observes, that the school and especially the university are institutions "cultivated and generously supported" by the (upper) middle class and organized to legitimize its authority (288, 123–24; Brint 34–36, 50–51, 83; Derber, Schwartz, and Magrass 82–92). It is to acknowledge, therefore, what one might call the liminal importance for the working class of reading books or, later on perhaps, wishing to write them. In a working-class milieu, a child's desire to read books or to succeed in school signifies difference—emotional, intellectual, and material difference. The working-class child who likes to read must leave the home and even the neighborhood to find novels or stories: she must get on her bike and pedal to the public library (if she is old enough and if, in these days of reduced municipal services, a library is open nearby), or she must convince her dismissive, perhaps even openly antagonistic parents to drive her there. She cannot just pick a novel off a shelf in her bedroom because in her own house, if she is lucky, the library consists of the Bible, *Reader's Digest, People,* and her neighbor's tattered *Tattler.*

In that house, in that culture, she looks for space, looks for privacy, looks for books—and finds none. Instead, she does her homework under bad light at the kitchen table, ignoring as best she can the noise that surrounds her. "My neighborhood was cacophonous with the noise of work and rage," writes Mary Cappello, now a professor of English at the University of Rhode Island. Men in her neighborhood were always working on something that was broken—cars, of course, but pipes or roofs or fences, too. Children were always playing outside, on the streets. People were always too close together: "When I try to picture the street I grew up on, my mind floods with the fear of impending violence, and all I hear is a heartbeat—but whose?—like the padding of feet down a corridor of no return. The violence of seeing and being seen. The violence of being forced to listen and being wholly heard. The violence of body opening body, of male against male or male against female" (186–87).

Books are liminally important, and the desire to read books or to succeed in school is seen by many as a betrayal of the values and the integrity of the working-class community. Working-class kids play sports or work on cars or take care of younger siblings; they don't read and study. Those who do, and who therefore do well in school, are sometimes ostracized by their peers, taunted or tormented on the playground or in the halls, and even by their families or parents: "Dad . . . used to hit me for *reading*," seethes an adult and dying Tom in Paul Monette's *Halfway Home* (19). In other instances, the working-class child who excels in school pays a price of shame and alienation with respect to her neighbors, friends, and parents, whose way of life she learns to disdain. In her autobiographical novel *Cleaned Out,* Annie Ernaux reveals that although her mother believed in books and "would have given me books to eat if she could have, . . . what she didn't realize was that these same books were shutting me off from her, taking me away from them and their cafe, showing me how awful it was" (77). Upward mobility indeed implies, if not requires, a value judgment: "those who climb up have a different sense of themselves and of their relationship to the world around them. . . . And whether they bear the lash of resentment of those they left behind, or the smile of approval of their newfound peers, the messages they get reinforce their self-image as not just different but better" (Rubin 9).

Concern for books, a concern for (in Guillory's phrase) "access to the means of literary production and consumption" is, then, like the school itself, part of (upper) middle-class culture, which is why, as Guillory himself suggests, the movement to open the canon has relatively little effect in altering structures of social inequality. What the open canon reveals, according to Guillory, is "the imaginary ego ideal of a newly constituted professional-managerial class, no longer exclusively white or male" (*Capital* 38). Efforts by women and minorities such as "opening the canon" are directed at "getting into the elite professions and managerial positions by following existing

career channels" (Collins, *Credential* 201)—the long haul through the educational system. But "making . . . abstract bureaucratic credentials easier . . . to
obtain" (*Credential* 130), which in turn makes it possible for some women
and minorities to enter elite professions, is obviously "an elitist reform that
will have little effect on the economic prospects" of the majority of those previously excluded (*Credential* 201). For these reasons, to change the structure
of inequality in the United States requires not the decoupling of the class
structure and the formation of cultural capital, as Guillory suggests, but
rather the decoupling of education and occupational opportunity. It
requires, as Collins suggests, "the abolition of credentialing" and the substitution of on-the-job training and recruitment for managerial and professional positions (*Credential* 202, 201).

It is perhaps needless to say that Collins is not hopeful about the possibility
of such a revolution: "it is far easier for allegedly liberal or even radical movements to continue the long-standing tradition of expanding access to the credential system" (*Credential* 203). Vicki Mahaffey broadens this insight, or
accounts for it, by suggesting that artistic or intellectual privilege is one "that
criticism, even 'resistant' criticism, may seek to redistribute but not to challenge" (668; Hoffman; Derber, Schwartz, and Magrass). As artists or intellectuals, even as dissident or oppositional artists or intellectuals, we have an interest
in maintaining the conditions that govern our privilege and authority. It is reasonable—and, perhaps, soothing—to "redistribute" intellectual privilege, to
open the university's doors to women or to members of minority groups who
resemble the white, male, (upper) middle-class norm, who write books and do
research.[3] It is unreasonable to "challenge" intellectual privilege by suggesting
that physical or manual labor be valued over (or even be valued as much as)
intellectual labor; or that occupational opportunity or mobility be based on
what goes on in the workplace rather than in schools; or that the cultural
choices of the working class be respected for revealing sound judgment and
taste. We cannot "open the canon" to working-class culture because working-
class culture is, traditionally, what we work to keep out and what the working
class works to overcome. As Frow observes, apparently with little regret, "there
are clear limits to the extent to which it is possible for intellectuals to associate
themselves with anti-intellectualism" (158).

Let me sum up what Councilman Littrell from my hometown seems to
intuit. For the working class, books take you away and distinguish you from
your peers; and they give you the power to judge others, or perhaps more accurately for most of the working class, books give others the power to judge you.
The professor, situated in the academy and perhaps the supreme warder of

books, institutionalizes subordination and thus class through her ability to evaluate, to pass on or to fail. The power of her authority, as Watkins emphasizes, "visibly and immediately seems to control the outcome of the situation and visits its humiliations on you" ("Intellectual" 208–9).

Shakespeare, who succeeded in letters despite his small Latin and less Greek, expresses these points well, in *The Tempest*. A look at Frank Kermode's influential introduction to the Arden edition of the play, first published in 1954 and still a standard scholarly edition, reveals among other things that Shakespeare's play is a pastoral romance, like Milton's *Comus* or book 6 of Spenser's *Faerie Queene*, and takes as one of its principal concerns the opposition of nature and art, the "great and perennial problem of the nature of Nature," a problem given contemporary force, new energy, by recent European exploration and colonization in the New World (xxv). What is the status of individuals or societies untainted by civilization? Are such "natural" individuals or societies uncorrupted? Or are they in many ways defective, requiring cultivation and improvement? Argument on the issue ranged widely: Montaigne, in "Of Cannibals," subscribed generally to the former view, while those invested in various colonial enterprises promoted the latter. Shakespeare developed a middle position, but one aligned with that of the colonialist: Caliban, Kermode assures us, "is the core of the play" in that he "is a measure of the incredible superiority of the world of Art, but also a measure of its corruption" (xxiv, xlii). What Shakespeare leads us to, Kermode implies, is an understanding of the ways to avoid such corruption: to control nature, the artist must exercise "virtue and temperance" and must liberate his "soul from the passions" (xlviii). Art, as honed and perfected by Prospero, "is the ordination of civility, the control of appetite, the transformation of nature by breeding and learning; it is even, in a sense, the means of Grace" (xlviii).

Or is it?

As Howard Felperin has pointed out, to subscribe nowadays to such a reading of *The Tempest* "would be to risk being demonized as 'idealist' or 'aestheticist' or 'essentialist'" (171), as indeed, in Felperin's judgment, Kermode was so judged in the 1980s by Francis Barker and Peter Hulme, among others (171 n. 2). Nevertheless, institutionalized by Kermode's introduction, this idealist reading dominated criticism for thirty years, until the mid-1970s, when critical focus shifted to problems of power in the play, particularly with respect to race and gender. One measure of the idealist reading's rapid and violent dismantling is that colleagues barely a decade older than I, colleagues in their midfifties, still subscribe to it. "I'm sick of hearing *The Tempest* is a colonialist document," more than one such colleague has complained to me—and I am not making this up for the sake of argument. Equally telling as a measure of the new reading's dominance is that a critic of my generation, Deborah Willis, has found it necessary, as Richard Halpern puts it in his own recent contribution to the ledger of colonialist readings, to spend "considerable polemical energy to arguing that *The Tempest might* be about something other than (or rather, something in addition to) colonialism" ("Nobody" 265n).[4]

Halpern also suggests that particularly in its new historicist form, "awareness of colonialism was, for the most part, forced onto Western intellectuals by the cultural, political, and military resistance of the colonized themselves. If we now cannot read *The Tempest* without seeing in it a drama of colonialism, we ultimately owe this insight to the work of O. Mannoni, Frantz Fanon, George Lamming, Roberto Fernández-Retamar, Aimé Césaire, and others" (*Moderns* 46). Doubtless Halpern is correct here, yet I am sure he would agree with Donald Pease (120–23) and Richard Wilson ("Voyage" 337) that new historicists have been interestingly selective in their use of the anticolonialists, and with Felperin that colonialist readings of *The Tempest* are not new: "what *Tempest* criticism is now experiencing is actually a *second* flowering of colonial allegorization," the flip side, so to speak, of the first, proimperial set of readings produced in the middle to late nineteenth century (176).

What strikes us about the colonialist readings since the mid-1970s, then, cannot be their newness: in 1972, Leslie Fiedler commended none other than Kermode for his adventurousness in supporting the insights of Fanon and Césaire and in helping to create a literary and theatrical culture in which "no respectable production of the play . . . can afford to ignore the sense in which it is a parable of transatlantic imperialism, the colonization of the West" (209).[5] Already in 1972, Fiedler implies, the critical tendency to see *The Tempest* as an American play was impeding other visions of it (209), a complaint resurrected in 1997 by Wilson: "it may be that the New Historicist success in relocating *The Tempest* in Virginia has transported it too far from Virgil, and the Old World of Aeneas where its action is set, between Tunis and Naples." What strikes us, then, about the current crop of colonialist readings is not just their numbers but their intensity and focus: Shakespeare's last comedy "has been Americanized . . . as a tragedy of colonialism in the New World" and as a tragedy of African slavery in the New World ("Voyage" 333).

But what strikes me, and what is significant, I hope, and not merely interesting or coincidental, is that critical interest in colonialist readings begins in the mid-1970s, just about the time that the play's value for African and

Caribbean intellectuals fades. In an oft-cited article, Rob Nixon has pointed out that the period of decolonialization, from roughly the late fifties to the early seventies, was an especially fruitful time for African and Caribbean intellectuals to use the play in efforts of personal and national self-definition (558). Yet in the postcolonial period, Nixon argues, *The Tempest* has held no such utility: "the play lacks a sixth act which might have been enlisted for representing relations among Caliban, Ariel, and Prospero once they entered a postcolonial era" (576). Nixon's explanation for that declining relevance focuses on the continuing domination of third world countries by former colonial powers: "Caliban's recovery of his island has proved a qualified triumph . . . [because] Prospero, having officially relinquished authority over the island, so often continues to manage it from afar" (576–77).

While Nixon's argument should be granted its due, one might also question why it elides as an explanation for "Caliban's . . . qualified triumph" what Ahmad insists is "the key fact about . . . post-colonial history . . . that each nation-state came under the dominance of a distinct national bourgeoisie (existing or emergent) as it emerged from the colonial crucible" (16). Indeed, Nixon invokes the problem of indigenous class division and conflict in order to dismiss it, a maneuver that requires some argumentative sleight of hand. Citing Marta Sanchez's essay in *Diacritics* for support, Nixon asserts that Roberto Fernández-Retamar's essay "Caliban," with its "distinctively Cuban" emphasis on the *mestizaje,* on the mulatto, recasts "the conflict between Prospero and Caliban . . . in class rather than racial terms" (575, 576). Yet Sanchez pointedly does not read Fernández-Retamar in this way. She specifically and at considerable length criticizes Fernández-Retamar for "stressing *mestizaje* rather than . . . class" in his assessments of Latin-American culture, for, as she explains

> the word *mestizaje* is general and vague. Essentially it refers to the *biological* mingling of *bloods.* The mixture of two or more different kinds of bloods, be they Black-Indian or Indian-White or Black-White, results in *mestizaje.* The term is not in any way meant to designate or even imply a *historical* struggle of *class.* In fact *mestizaje* is a sort of Latin-American "melting-pot" and has been used by the bourgeoisie to mythify Latin America's cultural heritage, thus supporting an evasion of a precise definition of race and class. Knowing this, we cannot help but suspect that Fernández-Retamar may be resorting to *mestizaje* for the evasive possibilities it offers . . . [collecting] the total of Latin America's inhabitants into the adjustable grab-bag of *mestizaje* that seems to accommodate everyone but in essence accommodates only those of the bourgeoisie who have proposed it as a panacea for the problems of Third World societies. (59–60)

What is interesting about Nixon's use of Sanchez in explicating Fernández-Retamar is not just that he gets her—and therefore him—wrong. Rather, it is that Nixon sees the decline of an intellectual movement, indeed its dissipation, in Fernández-Retamar's putative turn away from race and toward class, with its disturbing assertions about the intellectual who "can choose between serving Prospero . . . or allying himself with Caliban in his struggle for true freedom" (Fernández-Retamar 39).

As I have already noted, Nixon thinks *The Tempest* is unsuited "for representing relations among Caliban, Ariel, and Prospero once they entered a postcolonial era" (576). But if the problem of liberation in postcolonial societies is not exclusively with a Prospero who controls from afar, from London, Paris, or New York, then Nixon draws the wrong conclusion. If the problem of liberation in postcolonial societies is also the result of indigenous class divisions and conflict, if beneath the surface of racial oppression postcolonial history reveals the equally, if not more, intractable problem of class oppression, then *The Tempest* does not need a sixth act to hold relevance for a vital postcolonial intellectual movement, precisely to the extent that the play documents not only racial oppression but also class oppression and especially the role of education and of intellectuals in the creation and maintenance of it.

Several critics have nudged us toward this recognition. Stephen Orgel has commented that "in the New World, Europe could see its own past, itself in embryo" (44), a notion furthered by Terence Hawkes, who points out that "the roots of the Prospero-Caliban relationship extend beyond that of Planter to Slave to find their true nourishment in the ancient home-grown European relationships of master and servant, landlord and tenant" (*Rag* 3). And Stephen Greenblatt draws on Karen Kupperman's influential *Settling with the Indians* to suggest that Prince Hal's

> remark about drinking with any tinker in his own language suggests, if only jocularly, that for him the lower classes are virtually another people, an alien tribe—immensely more populous than his own—within the kingdom. That this perception extended beyond the confines of Shakespeare's play is suggested by the evidence that middle- and upper-class English settlers in the New World regarded the American Indians less as another race than as a version of their own lower classes; one man's tinker is another man's Indian. (*Negotiations* 49)

The notion that in *The Tempest* "art" or books or knowledge produces and institutionalizes class distinction and hierarchy is what I would like to explore in the next few pages, and I would strongly affirm, with Annabel Patterson, that "it does no dishonour to the anti-colonialist argument to suggest that *The Tempest* speaks to a still more expansive set of problems" (*Voice* 156). Yet I do wish to question most of those who make the argument: why should a turn toward class analysis be seen as a sign of intellectual dissipation? What does the exclusive and aggressively eager focus on racism and colonialism in *The Tempest* allow mostly white, upper-middle-class American literary critics to avoid both in the play and, more importantly, in their own lives?

In a sense, this argument is perfectly obvious: of course knowledge is power, and those who do not have access to either do not need Michel Foucault to enlighten them. And of course, Prospero's books are what allow him mastery on the island—as Caliban knows, "his Art is of such pow'r / It would control my dam's god, Setebos, / And make a vassal of him" (I.ii.374–76). Yet critics, and even critics who offer progressive, anticolonialist readings of the play, tend to indulge in revealing slippages: Prospero's hegemony, his "imposition of hierarchy upon difference," as Felperin calls it (174), is the result of colonialism, imperialism, sexism, racism, or capitalism, anything, in fact, except what the play patently reveals as the source of Prospero's power: book learnin'.

In this play about an intellectual, Shakespeare saves until the second scene the work of exposition. The first scene, in contrast, offers an image of men struggling unsuccessfully to master nature's power. In so arranging his scenes, Shakespeare violently calls into question his society's vision of hierarchical order, its division of men into those who labor and those—a privileged few— who do not. With the ship in grave danger, the idle aristocrats, including Alonzo, the King of Naples, emerge on deck in order to inquire nervously about their safety. The boatswain, busy at work, politely asks that they return to their cabins—"I pray now, keep below" (11). Insisting on their prerogative, the aristocrats ignore his request, and as the violence of the storm increases, making his work more difficult and dangerous, the boatswain becomes enraged and, violating the requirements of hierarchy, shouts to the King and his attendants:

> What cares these roarers
> for the name of King? . . .
>
> if you can command these elements to silence, and work
> the peace of the presence, we will not hand a rope more; use your author-
> ity: if you cannot, give thanks you have lived so long, and make yourself
> ready in your cabin for the mischance of the hour, if it so hap.
> . . . Out of our way, I say.
>
> (ll. 16–17, 21–27)

The boatswain is only partially successful. Within a few lines, the aristocrats again emerge on deck, and with the ship about to go down, the King's brother Sebastian curses and vilifies the hardworking boatswain, who, in response, hurls a pregnant challenge at the aristocrats: "Work you, then" (l. 42).

Neither idle aristocrats nor laboring mariners can master the storm; and, like Miranda, the audience or reader begins scene ii fearing that "a brave vessel . . . [is] dash'd all to pieces" (ll. 5–7). What can master the storm, we immediately discover, is Prospero's "art," his learning. Prospero assures Miranda that the wreck has been

> with such provision in mine Art
> So safely ordered, that there is no soul—
> No, not so much perdition as an hair
> Betid to any creature in the vessel
> Which thou heard'st cry, which thou saw'st sink.
>
> I.ii.28–32)

This is impressive power, indeed, as Caliban recognizes. Prospero's slave may be a "dull thing," one on whom "any print of goodness will not take" (I.ii.285, 354), but he is smart enough to know where Prospero's power lies and to instruct Stephano and Trinculo in a strategy for overthrowing him:

> 'tis a custom with him
> I' th' afternoon to sleep: there thou mayst brain him,
> Having first seiz'd his books; or with a log
> Batter his skull, or paunch him with a stake,
> Or cut his wezand with thy knife. Remember
> First to possess his books; for without them
> He's but a sot, as I am, nor hath not
> One spirit to command: they all do hate him
> As rootedly as I. Burn but his books.
>
> (III.ii.85–93)

"Burn but his books," for surely it is Prospero's books that enable him to control and humiliate those around him, and Caliban in particular. Books give Prospero "a fatal advantage over them all" (Fiedler 238), allowing him to inflict physical punishment on anyone who disobeys him: "tonight," says Prospero to Caliban, "thou shalt . . . be pinch'd / As thick as honeycomb, each pinch more stinging / Than bees that made 'em" (I.ii.327–32). In *The Tempest,* Fiedler noted almost thirty years ago, books are "symbols of a literate technology with which the ruling classes of Europe controlled the subliterates of two worlds," one old and the other new (238).

Patterson rightly suggests that *The Tempest* makes explicit "one of the central problems of populism: what is the role of education in political society, and what does it contribute to social justice?" She, too, cites Caliban's lines cited above, in identifying "hegemony's central dilemma—that while the educational system and its central symbol, *the book,* normally works to keep the underprivileged unenlightened, it occasionally produces, precisely by making them articulate, effective popular spokesmen" (*Voice* 157). Yet while acknowledging the "vexed status of literacy in the history of popular protest," as one must question the efficacy of an instrument that produces such poor results, Patterson implies that Caliban wants that power, the power of the articulate, because he "instructs Stephano and Trinculo to begin their insurrection by seizing Prospero's library" (*Voice* 157, 158). But Caliban's instructions, you will recall, are rather more radical—or are they more reactionary?—than that. Caliban does not want to possess Prospero's knowledge so that he can become properly bourgeois, or even, potentially, a fit mate for Miranda; nor, it seems, does he wish to become an effective popular spokesman. He wants something more elemental; he wants the knowledge that enslaves human beings erased from the earth, "not just the substitution of one master for another but the annihilation of all authority and all culture, a world eternally without slaves and clowns" (Fiedler 238). Stephano and Trinculo must seize, possess, and burn those books. Seize, possess, burn; it is populism's message, the message of those who distrust and resent both educated and moneyed elites, elites who presume, paternalistically, to determine for the masses what is in its best interests.

Of course, Prospero's books prove impossible to burn or even to possess, and despite Prospero's retirement, his vow to break his staff and drown his book, relations of power and privilege in *The Tempest* remain structurally unchanged. (Miranda is, after all, charted to become queen of Naples and Milan. And Caliban, still in servitude, resolves to "be wise hereafter, / And seek for grace" [V.i.294–95].) Still, it pleases me to think that Shakespeare enjoyed mocking the structure of power on which privilege depends in this play. With far less effort and cost than education, alcohol will make the unenlightened articulate, as Stephano, bearing sack, assures Caliban: "Come on your ways; open your mouth; here is that which will give language to you, cat: open your mouth" (II.ii.84–86). And in this play about the power of books, Shakespeare gives us an "abhorred slave" who succinctly anatomizes the uses of education for most workers: "You taught me language; and my profit on't / Is, I know how to curse" (I.ii.365–66). Consider the construction workers, putting up another monument to a moneyed philanthropist on our campus. What might they say after watching us shape the minds of undergraduates? Perhaps this Calibanism: "damned inte-fuckin'-lectuals."

It pleases me to think that Shakespeare enjoyed assessing the costs of book learning, and not just the benefits, as Kermode and even Patterson would have it. Shakespeare created an intellectual who, "neglecting worldly ends, all dedicated / To closeness and the bettering of my mind / With that which . . . / O'erpriz'd all popular rate," brings his dukedom to a sad condition, "to most ignoble stooping" (I.ii.89–92, 116). He created an intellectual whose behavior throughout the play verges on the tyrannical, prompting apologies from Miranda (I.ii.498–501) and a plea for tenderness from Ariel (V.i.17–19). In so doing, *The Tempest* offers us, as intellectuals, salutary warnings about the limits of the power of our art, our learning, and about the necessity of acknowledging or owning up to those whose difference defines us, as indeed Prospero finally acknowledges Caliban (V.i.275–76).

Such a reading is of special importance in America at the turn of the millennium, where the pain of working-class Americans is drawing increased attention, if still mostly in the popular press. In five years, between 1978 and 1982, high-paying manufacturing jobs were lost at a rate of almost one million per year (Beaty 68); millions more like them have been lost since then. In industries or locales where jobs were not lost, wages went down: in the 1980s, blue-collar and service-industry workers saw their wages drop significantly, by 12 percent and 18.2 percent, respectively (Mishel and Frankel 75). And worse, between 1974 and 1995, we have witnessed "not only a sizable growth in the proportion of workers earning poverty-level wages," increasing from about 24 percent in 1979 to almost 30 percent in 1995, but also a "significant expansion of workers earning far less than poverty-level wages." In 1979, only 4.2 percent of workers earned "wages at least 25% below the poverty-level wage"; in 1995, that number reached almost 15 percent (Mishel, Bernstein, and Schmitt 149). Family income has increased principally because wives have entered the labor force or because a head of household has taken a second or third job. The upshot is that it has become increasingly difficult for the 75 percent of "workers without a college degree to earn a middle class standard of living" (Mishel and Frankel 7).

The freefall in wages and benefits hurts the young and the non-college-educated most: Mishel, Bernstein, and Schmitt calculate that "the wages of the average non-college-educated male fell 10.1% from 1979 to 1989 and another 7.2% between 1989 and 1995. The wages of a young male high school graduate dropped 21.8% in the 1980s and another 6.9% in the 1989–95 period. A young female high school graduate earned 18.9% less in 1995 than in 1979" (18). In *Inequality by Design,* Fischer et al. paint a similar picture by putting the matter just a bit differently: "During the 1980s the hourly wage (adjusted for inflation) went up 13 percent for men who had graduated college but declined 8 percent for men who had dropped out of college, dropped 13 percent for men who had only graduated from high school, and plummeted 18 percent for male high school dropouts" (116). In short, except for the highly educated who hold down white-collar professional or managerial jobs, workers in the 1990s worked harder and longer for less money and fewer benefits.

In such a milieu—in which the United States, under a Democratic president, developed the most unequal distribution of income of any advanced industrial country (Fischer et al. 121; Mishel, Bernstein, and Schmitt 394) and in which the loss of high-paying blue-collar jobs intensifies an already obvious trend toward inequality by education (cf. Mishel, Bernstein, and Schmitt 168–75)—it is imperative that professors of English, like Prospero, acknowledge the value and worth not only of those with whom we succeed, like Ariel, but also of those whom we fail, those, like Caliban, on whom "any print of goodness wilt not take" and "on whose nature / Nurture can never stick" (I.ii.354, IV.i.188–89). Deindustrialization and the development of a global economy suggest that the numbers of those who will fail must increase dramatically, yet there appears to be little interest in acknowledging them or their value and worth. We seem content that there is not "a lot of positive validation of low-income peoples' abilities in this society" (Croteau 139).

So content are we that we have replaced those disappointing losers, the working class, as the "privileged agent in which the fundamental impulse of social change resides" (Laclau and Mouffe 177). Women, people of color, homosexuals, environmentalists, peace activists—these are the groups now privileged by the Left. Yet it is significant that these newly privileged agents of social change are, in fact, quite similar to upper-middle-class intellectuals. They press their claims via new social movements (NSMs), whose memberships tend overwhelmingly to be highly educated and (upper) middle class (Croteau 11; Brint 199–201). Unlike older class or workers' movements, NSMs are social rather than political in nature, aiming not to redesign the state but to work within it in the "piecemeal defence of particular threatened groups or lifestyles" and advancing these "narrower causes" via strategies of cultural or symbolic (ex)change: "bringing them to public notice, engaging in persuasive argumentation on their behalf, and claiming not power and submission but space and tolerance" (Barnes 161; Brint 199). Some theorists, such as Alvin Gouldner or George Konrád and Ivan Szelényi, "have even argued that new social movements were created in part to advance the interests of a 'knowledge' class. . . , providing them with a space to unite technical expertise with humanistic orientations" (Croteau 164). Certainly, with their deep ties to the (upper) middle class, new social movements allow intellectuals to focus on politics by avoiding institutional and social locations other than their own.

For literary critics, this insularity of political practice arguably results from the tendency of literary theory to offer a "decisively culturalist figuration of political and social power," which is perhaps why Francis Barker insists that "the difference between the aestheticisation of politics and the politicisation of aesthetics remains crucial" (165, 201 n. 60). Pease contends that the failure to maintain this distinction allows, for example, the new historicist "to misrecognize the colonialist practices that the new historicism symbolically continues—as if they are subversive of the colonialist enterprise" ("Sociology" 137). I contend that the failure to maintain this distinction allows literary critics to misrecognize intrainstitutional maneuverings on behalf of or via women, people of color, homosexuals, and so on, which most versions of literary theory, not just new historicism, symbolically continue—as if they are subversive of institutional power, or social power more generally. Thus the concern with racism, colonialism, imperialism, sexism, or capitalism in *The Tempest* and elsewhere allows us to avoid our own deep responsibility for inequality in this society, the fact that we, as much or more so than capitalists, produce and reproduce inequality.[6]

Consider, for example, Robbins's "Oppositional Professionals: Theory and the Narratives of Professionalization," which sets out to argue that "the words 'oppositional' and 'professional' are not antithetical" (4). For Robbins, this is an important point largely because he has decided that our professional status is a fact about which we can do nothing (3, 4). Despite wide reading in the history and sociology of professions, Robbins seems to ignore the principal arguments and motivation of Bledstein, Collins, and Larson, all of whom he cites and all of whom wish to understand how and why professionalization (in league with credentialing) instituted and maintained a new and dominant form of structured inequality in the nineteenth and twentieth centuries. Robbins finds in the university the "conditions of possibility" for oppositionality (4) and takes comfort in the notion that it is "oppositional" to change (slightly) the gender and racial makeup of the limited and elite minority who may share in its discourse (17–19). In doing so, Robbins fails to acknowledge not only the extent to which, as Larson points out, a professional group "*must* appeal to general values of the dominant ideology if it is to make its own values acceptable" (*Rise* 157) but also the extent to which, as Brint repeatedly insists, higher education in

particular "primarily encourages responsiveness to whatever stands as the pre-
vailing climate of opinion among political elites" (109; 14, 117–18, 168). Robbins
thereby cannot acknowledge the extent to which, rather than contest dominant
ideology, "professionalism . . . makes an important contribution to the ideological denial of structural inequality" (Larson, *Rise* 156).

That role has not gone unnoticed by workers, who on the one hand have
good reason to be anti-intellectual and on the other hand—if, in conclusion, I
may broaden my scope—have good reason to question current affirmative
action policies in colleges and universities. Commentators have suggested that
affirmative action is sticky and difficult because it is a symbolic issue; as opponents of affirmative action point out, the policy undermines American notions
of equal opportunity and advancement according to merit. In response,
defenders of affirmative action point out that, for example, admissions policies
at colleges and universities have never been based solely on merit; athletes,
musicians, children of alumni, and in particular children of alumni donors are
given preference routinely. Admissions policies, say the defenders, have always
been strongly mediated. No one has so far suggested that if affirmative action
be eliminated for minorities and women, it also be eliminated for basketball
players or opera singers as surely as for Kennedys and Bushes; it is likely no one
will.[7] But I will suggest that affirmative action for minorities and women is a
flash point because it brings to the public's attention an uncomfortable fact, the
fact I have been discussing in this chapter, which is the basic contradiction in
the American educational system: in the United States, intellectual merit—
defined as success in the (upper) middle-class institution of the school—is
used to justify class inequality and the reproduction of class inequality.

Thus, even as elite universities and colleges, both private and public, have
become more racially diverse, they have become more economically homoge-
neous. Concludes a 1989 report to the Berkeley Division of the Academic Senate at the University of California: "while Berkeley has made considerable
progress on diversifying the racial and ethnic composition of its student body,
it has made remarkably little progress in diversifying the socioeconomic composition of the freshmen class." In 1987, when the national median family
income was approximately $30,000, the median family income of entering stu-
dents at Berkeley was $53,000. Fifty-five percent of entering students reported
incomes over $50,000 and 27 percent over $75,000 (Karabel et al. 43). At Berkeley's sister institution UCLA, the figures four years later were, not surprisingly,
even higher: over 60 percent of entering freshmen at UCLA reported family
incomes over $60,000, and 24 percent reported over $100,000 (Jacoby 21).

Not only, then, has income inequality increased in the United States since the 1970s, so that, as mentioned above, the United States now suffers the most unequal income distribution of any advanced industrial country, but so, too, has educational inequality. After all, asks Todd Gitlin, "who can afford the price of admission?" There is a "growing polarization between those who benefit from higher education and those who do not": in 1979, a student whose family's income fell in the top quarter was four times as likely to earn a bachelor's degree by age twenty-four as a student whose family's income fell in the bottom quarter. By 1994, such an affluent student was nineteen times as likely to do so (*Dream* 225). Russell Jacoby finds

> the gentrification of higher education . . . troubling. Everyone applauds the ethnic and racial diversity of American campuses, visible in faces and skin hues. . . . Yet within the augmented ethnic diversity exists its opposite, an augmented affluent homogeneity; even as the students are more different, they are more alike. (27)

Indeed, concludes Gitlin, "this is class division with a vengeance" (*Dream* 225), and it is class division, or inequality, that is caused by a stratified system of education.

In the next chapter, "Aping Aristocrats," I turn my focus to the target most routinely attacked and demonized by intellectuals for causing inequality, capitalism and the market. I offer reasons for this demonization that are rooted in intellectual and professional self-interest, rather than moral selflessness.

CHAPTER THREE

Aping Aristocrats

Timon of Athens and the Anticapitalism of Intellectuals

*I*n explaining to Roderigo why he continues to serve Othello when he no longer feels "in any just term . . . affin'd / To love the Moor," Iago distinguishes between two kinds of servants and two kinds of service:

> You shall mark
> Many a duteous and knee-crooking knave,
> That, doting on his own obsequious bondage,
> Wears out his time much like his master's ass,
> For nought but provender, and when he's old, cashier'd,
> Whip me such honest knaves: others there are,
> Who, trimm'd in forms, and visages of duty,
> Keep yet their hearts attending on themselves,
> And throwing but shows of service on their lords,
> Do well thrive by 'em, and when they have lin'd their coats,
> Do themselves homage, those fellows have some soul,
> And such a one do I profess myself.
>
> (*Othello* I.i. 44–55)

Because of the injury endured in being passed over for promotion, a promotion that "by the old gradation" should have been his, Iago no longer feels bound to love the Moor, and thus redefines his relationship to service and to Othello, casting himself as a fellow with some soul, who serves in order to thrive, to get ahead personally, as he reiterates to the somewhat skeptical Roderigo: "In following him, I follow but myself. / Heaven is my judge, not I for love and duty, / But seeming so, for my peculiar end" (I.i.58–60).

Not for love and duty does Iago serve, but several years earlier, Shakespeare created—and, it is believed, enacted on the stage—a character who embodies "The constant service of the antique world, / When service sweat for duty, not for meed" (*As You Like It* II.iii.57–58). Old Adam not only warns Orlando of his brother's evil plottings, thereby putting his own safety in question, but also offers the impoverished younger brother his entire life's savings to stead him in his escape,

> five hundred crowns,
> The thrifty hire I sav'd under your father,
> Which I did store to be my foster-nurse
> When service should in my old limbs lie lame,
> And unregarded age in corners thrown.

(II.iii.38–42)

Adam's loyalty and utter selflessness—his uncomplaining acknowledgment that the fate Iago abhors is likely to be his—prompt Orlando to lament the

> fashion of these times,
> Where none will sweat but for promotion,
> And having that, do choke their service up
> Even with the having.

(II.iii.59–62)

Orlando and Iago describe the kinds of service in the same way—one rooted in duty and one in self-interest; and similar oppositions occur in other plays. Consider, for example, the contrast between the loyal servants of Timon and the "base" self-interested servants of Timon's flatterers in *Timon of Athens* (e.g. III.i.43–52, III.iv.40–60, and IV.ii); or that between Oswald and Kent in *King Lear*, one of whom proves himself to be "super-serviceable" in the effort "to raise [his] fortunes" and one of whom knows how, in seeking service, to recognize "authority" in the "countenance" of one he "would fain call master" (II.ii.16–17, IV.vi.225, I.iv.27–30).

All this is not simply a matter of good servants and bad, an early-seventeenth-century lament about the difficulty of finding good help these days. Something else is going on here, a signifier of change in a society in which service was both routine and socially significant. "One nearly always 'belonged' to somebody," as Philippe Ariès observes (396), but such a relationship was not just personal: it implied an identification with a specific social institution (Stallybrass 290). Taking a cue from Stephen Greenblatt, therefore, I would suggest that in Shakespeare's representations of service, we find more evidence that early modern "status relations . . . are being transformed before our eyes into property relations" ("Peasants" 25). It is a transformation—or a social ambiguity—that Shakespeare, as actor, would have experienced personally. Actors avoided being categorized as masterless men by submitting to the authority of the nobility; yet according to David Scott Kastan, the "structure of service . . . existed more as legal fiction than social fact. The companies of players that nominally existed in the household of some great lord in fact functioned on a clear commercial basis, dependent on their patron only for the right to function professionally" (108).

In such representations of service, Shakespeare responds to the beginnings of a process that, roughly two hundred years later, with the making of the English working class, largely severs the reciprocal bonds of connection, the lasting dependencies, between inferiors and superiors that organized society and inequality before the industrial revolution. Shakespeare responds to a process that slowly transforms service, and labor more generally, from a matter of social relations to a matter of economics, a process Zygmunt Bauman has called a "de-socialisation" of labor (103). Labor so conceived required submission for wages only: subordinates would arrange for their own security out of their wages, and masters would suffer the not insubstantial grievances of a free labor force (102).

Of course, even when a relationship is rearticulated in principle or theory, it is not necessarily or immediately rearticulated in practice; such rearticulation is a social process requiring education and discipline, as Bauman recognizes (102). Both masters and subordinates clung to feudal assumptions and expectations, even though in principle neither could claim what was their due within the feudal relation—deference, loyalty, and love for the one, and security, protection, and assistance for the other. The transition to capitalism is one "in which pre-capitalist forms (and orders) are maintained and reproduced" (Beynon 248). As late as the mid–nineteenth century, many capitalists in England "were strongly committed to the ideas of paternalism and to a view of society based upon status and obligation" (246). And, perhaps more surprisingly, "considerable evidence" suggests that such commitment was "also present within the growing numbers of industrial workers," especially with respect to occupational cultures (247, 248; Bauman 100–112). What Huy Beynon's research implies is summed up nicely by Keith Wrightson: "class was not born at the turn of the eighteenth and nineteenth centuries, any more than hierarchy died" (200).

For criticism, what is at issue is how to theorize inequality, that is, relationships between superiors and subordinates within Shakespeare's plays, and not incidentally, of course, within early modern England. Certainly, we can detect

in the literature of the period evidence of a new concern with personal property—in this case, with the ownership of the servant's labor. As Marx points
out in *Capital,* the worker could sell his own labor "only after he had ceased to
be bound to the soil, and ceased to be the slave or serf of another person. To
become a free seller of labor-power, who carries his commodity wherever he
can find a market for it, he must further have escaped from the regime of the
guilds, their rules for apprentices and journeymen, and their restrictive labor
regulations" (875).[1] Yet it is also clear that this is a society organized as a network or web of dependencies, of rights and obligations: *The Courtier* provides
essential information about success, and what passes for a monetary economy
is primarily the exchange of "gifts, perks, and favors" (Stallybrass 291). With
respect to service, there existed between masters and servants throughout the
seventeenth century "something which went beyond respect for a contract or
exploitation by an employer: an existential bond which did not exclude brutality on the one hand and cunning on the other, but which resulted from an
almost perpetual community of life" (Ariès 396; Elias, *Court;* Bauman).

Such a "perpetual community of life" is quite obvious in Shakespeare's
many representations of the master-servant relationship. One thinks of "servants" whose positions are not low and who are themselves empowered to
command others, such as Malvolio in *Twelfth Night,* the steward in *Timon of
Athens,* Cassio and Iago in *Othello,* Kent and Oswald in *King Lear,* or Enobar-
bus in *Antony and Cleopatra.* One thinks, too, of servants whose positions are
complicated by a location within a family or household, such as the nurse in
Romeo and Juliet, Grumio in *The Taming of the Shrew,* and the twin Dromios in
The Comedy of Errors. Representations such as these approve the period's continual analogizing of the master-servant relationship to that of the husband
and wife, or parent and child (Cressy 29–44; Ariès 365–407).

The master-servant relationship in Shakespeare's plays, then, is not defined
exclusively or even generally in terms of economic domination and exploitation. As the examples cited above suggest, domination is less abstract, embed-
ded as it is within hierarchies of household and family, of the military, or of the
state. Furthermore, Shakespeare's plays cast as evil those servants who, like
Iago or Oswald, wish to break the bonds of a "perpetual community of life" and
redefine service as primarily an economic relationship, as an exchange of labor
for resources that allow personal advancement. We are led, generally, to prefer
the old Adams and the Kents of the canon to the Iagos or the Oswalds, and to
laugh at the brutality that molds the loyal servant, the beatings endured by a
Grumio or a Dromio. For reasons like these, Shakespeare's plays pose difficulty

for critics who, in addressing inequality and subordination in them, look primarily to Marx and Marxian class analysis for interpretive help or theoretical grounding, thereby ignoring or discounting the established and competing model of stratification in the early modern period, that is, one revealed in a hierarchy of status, in which an economy of prestige takes precedence over an economy of money.[2]

This theoretical difficulty appears often in the critical literature. Consider, for example, a contribution to *Shakespeare Quarterly* that ponders "the representation of 'class'" in scenes from *The Taming of the Shrew, The Merchant of Venice,* and *Julius Caesar.* In this essay, Thomas Moisan opens his discussion of these scenes by acknowledging the existence of competing models of social stratification, one rooted in status and the other rooted in class. As the essay proceeds, however, and as the title suggests, Moisan gives precedence to the latter model, or at least, he allows status to be absorbed by class (276). More recently, Kastan has offered another and more slippery account of relationships between status and class. Beginning by admitting that class analysis of early modern social relations is, strictly speaking, an anachronism, Kastan works to find a less strict way of speaking. In the hope of concluding (which, in fact, he does) that class "can be more or less happily accepted as an effective heuristic, if not a properly historical category" for the analysis of early modern literature and social relations (102), Kastan develops the following argument: early modern "social vocabularies of 'estate' or 'degree,' while insisting on social differentiation on the basis of status rather than on the basis of income and occupation, no less powerfully testify to a system of social inequality that the concept of class would help articulate and analyze" (101).

What Kastan seems to insist upon is that to analyze social inequality based on status, which is distinguishable from that based on income and occupation, one should use a vocabulary of class, which is well tuned to describe the latter, rather than the early modern vocabulary of estates and degrees, which is well tuned to describe the former. One should do this, Kastan claims, for heuristic reasons. Perhaps; but explanation suffers when definitional slipperiness results in sequences of sentences like these:

> The constitutive role-playing of the theater demystifies the idealization of the social order that the ideology of degree would produce. The successful counterfeiting of social rank raises the unnerving possibility that social rank is a counterfeit, existing "but as the change of garments" in a play, in Walter Ralegh's telling phrase. In the theaters of London, if not in the *the-*

atrum mundi, class positions are exposed as something other than essential facts of human existence, revealed, rather, as changeable and constructed. (106–7)

In these lines, "degree," "social rank," and "class positions" are synonymous. Kastan's happy reliance on a loose "abstract social sense" of class, which allows him to cast it as synonymous with degree and rank, obscures the actual (ideological) workings of inequality in social formations that stratify by class and by status. The effects of status inequality do need to be exposed as "something other than essential facts of human existence"; the effects of class inequality do not need—and indeed cannot have—such exposure, for in its strict analytic sense, which Kastan eschews, class is by definition constructed and changeable, rooted as it is in one's relation to the means of production.

Later on in the essay, Kastan associates class not with income and occupation but with wealth. Regarding sumptuary legislation (which regulated social cross-dressing in early modern England, regulations actors routinely violated onstage), Kastan asserts that an instability in "social identities and relations" is

in part constituted by the contradictory definition of status, as in the proclamation, both in terms of rank (a knight or baron) and in terms of wealth ("such as may dispend £200 by the year"). This contradiction reveals the vulnerability of the traditional culture based on hierarchy and deference to the transformative entrepreneurial energies of a nascent capitalism. (105–6)

But in 1983, Lisa Jardine found no such contradictory definition of status in the sumptuary proclamation, since "the 'net income' categories stipulate that income should be 'per year for life', once again excluding those without income-producing investments, that is, landholdings" (145). Although I would lay my bet with Jardine, my immediate concern is not whether Jardine or Kastan is correct here, since in any case, both identify a tension between rank and wealth in the sumptuary legislation. My point is that a tension between rank and wealth is not equivalent to a tension between rank and class, regardless of the origins of the wealth in landholdings or entrepreneurial activity. Capitalist activity is something one may do with wealth (and if it is done on a large-enough scale perhaps eventually will result in a system of stratification by class); wealth is a necessary but not sufficient condition for either capitalism or class. To move from "entrepreneurial energies of a nascent capitalism" to wealth to class, as Kastan does implicitly, is to empty out the meaning of each of these terms. But then, this move seems to be Kastan's intention: "It may well be . . . that any anxiety about the deployment of the language of class in the discussion of Shakespeare's plays is an unnecessary scruple" (101). By emptying out the definitions, Kastan empties out his own anxiety about unnecessary scruples.

Kastan is much more accurate and useful, I believe, when he does not treat class and status as synonyms, as in these lines from later in the essay: "If it isn't quite accurate to say that the theater, with its imitative disruption of the traditional culture of status, brought that culture to an end, certainly the theater's conspicuous presence signaled its vulnerability to dissolution in the transformative energies of the nascent capitalism of early modern England; and if it isn't quite accurate to say that the entrepreneurial successes of the acting companies actually brought 'class' into being, certainly in the visible signs of their abundant energies and aspirations they brought class into view" (114). Here Kastan keeps class and status analytically distinct (one cannot substitute class for status, even a loose definition of it, and maintain meaning in the sentence); and he implies thereby a certain historical relationship between modes of inequality or stratification that carry with them a range of cultural consequences. As I argued in chapter 1 and will develop here, stratification by class and stratification by status are logically and analytically (not to mention actually) different; each form of stratification brings into being different sorts of winners and losers, good guys and bad, oppressors and oppressed; and it ought to be a matter of debate as to which institutionalization of inequality is to be preferred and under which circumstances.

To engage in such debate, one must be (at least reasonably) strict in describing the ways class stratifies and the ways status stratifies. The winners and losers in a status society (or in a class society, for that matter) cannot be well described by a concept so loosely defined that it becomes a synonym for winners and losers in general, as in Kastan's assertion that "classes, in their abstract social sense, can be seen to have existed as long as social organization has permitted an unequal distribution of property, privilege, and power" (101). Therefore, it is precisely what Kastan rejects, the modern "economic definition" of class, that is useful to us in attempting to analyze the "system of social inequality" that Kastan and I agree exists in the early modern period.

Part of my argument, to which I turn toward the end of this chapter, concerns such slippages as those endorsed by Moisan and Kastan: what are the political—and intellectual—implications of literary critics' generally failing to distinguish between class and status as concepts, turning them virtually into synonyms? First, though, let me return to the suggestion that Kastan gives up the fight for a strict use of class too easily. Stratification based on class is not irrelevant to the early modern period. Class as a principle of stratification is, however, "emerging" at this time; the transformation of England into a class society has barely begun,[3] and takes, perhaps, another 200 to 250 years to achieve, during which time elements of the status order remained intact and influential, as some do today. Any given social formation—or at least any social formation that includes market institutions—will differentiate by status and by class; differentiation by class and by status coexist, to different degrees and strengths in differing times and places. The point, as argued in chapter 1, is not to subsume status by class or to see the relationships between them as "in conflict" or as emergent and residual, but to assess the relative strength of each, while keeping in mind the possibilities of tension between them or that they may coincide or overlap. John R. Hall has phrased the question thus: "What is the interaction between markets and groups, between class and status, between economic formations and cultural formations?" (277). To tease out such inter-action, Hall insists, as I do above, that it is necessary to "maintain an analytic distinction between status group and class" (273). What follows is additional work toward making that distinction, which builds upon my discussion in chapter 1. I then turn to a brief discussion of *Timon of Athens* and its criticism.

Class is a form of stratification that can be distinguished from other forms of stratification, such as those based on kinship, caste, or status. All societies are stratified or ranked according to some criterion or another, either alone or in concert; inequality is nothing new and neither is a concentration of power in the hands of a privileged few. Within capitalist or market societies the domi-nant but by no means exclusive form of stratification is class, a form of stratification in which privilege is determined by one's role in the processes of production, that is, by one's relationship to the means of production of goods. For Marx, class signifies conflict: Ralf Dahrendorf emphasizes that in the Marx-ian sense, class does not offer a snapshot of hierarchy in a society at a given point in time but involves the attempt to understand social conflict or the pos-sibilities for organized action (76). Not that conflict is unique to capitalist soci-ety, for as Bauman points out, feudal society "had also its language of conflict." But capitalist society moves "conflict from the murky, shadowy, and threaten-ing margins of the social order into the very centre of society; from the scrap heap to the main building site of social order" (39).

Implicit in this analysis is the notion that economic relations determine social and political development. This notion has been difficult for some to accept, and perhaps the first theorist to attack Marx on this score was Max

Weber, much of whose sociology is, according to Giddens, "an attack upon the Marxian generalisation that class struggles form the main dynamic process in the development of society" (50). Although Weber agrees with much that Marx has to say about class in general and with respect to conflict within industrial capitalism, Weber takes issue particularly with Marx's insistence that a class— *those with common economic situations* within a nation (or even across nations)—necessarily would develop class consciousness, move from a class in itself to a class for itself, and thus become principal agents within history. For Weber, "'classes' are not communities; they merely represent possible, and frequent, bases for social action," which may take any of "innumerable possible forms" or none at all: "the emergence of an association or even of mere social action from a common class situation is by no means a universal phenomenon" (927, 930, 929).

In short, Weber thinks Marx greatly exaggerates the role of economic relations in the development of modern societies and in the operations of power within them. Weber argues that for "'class action' (social action by members of a class)" to occur,

> the real conditions and the results of the class situation must be distinctly recognizable. For only then the contrast of life chances can be felt not as an absolutely given fact to be accepted, but as a resultant from either (1) the given distribution of property, or (2) the structure of the concrete economic order. It is only then that people may react against the class structure not only through acts of intermittent and irrational protest, but in the form of rational association. (929)

What Weber suggests is that it simply is not likely, as Collins points out, for "all the members of a Marxian class—essentially reifications of the abstract factors of production in economic theory—to act together as a unified group" (*Theory* 129). For class action to occur there must be, essentially, some social glue, a community or association, a network of communication and interaction, of sanction and praise, of distinctive lifestyle and exclusivity that flows from cultural groupings such as those based in religion, ethnicity, education, or professional skill.

Social theorists in the Weberian tradition emphasize that the existence of cultural or status groups "does not eliminate class conflict." Status groups on this view enable class conflict because they offer "the natural form in which economic interests can act socially" (Collins, *Theory* 129; Barnes 130ff.). Weber thus insists that the "cultural" and the "political" influence the structure of power far more than Marx allows, and Fredric Jameson locates "Weber's most influential legacy to the anti-Marxist arsenal" in precisely this "strategic substitution, in his own research and theorization, of the political for the economic realm as the principal object of study, and thus, implicitly, as the ultimately determining reality of history" (4).

Weber argues that what is definitive and radical about capitalism is not the emergence of classes but its rationalized production. In this, capitalism follows the lead of the state, itself already rationalized and bureaucratized; for Weber, "the trend towards the expansion of bureaucratisation expresses the integral character of the modern epoch: the rationalisation of human conduct creates a systematised and hierarchical division of labour which is not directly dependent upon the capitalist class structure" (Giddens 46). Jameson thinks Weber (or a Weberian perspective) displaces questions of the economy onto political and social history such that, for example, "analyses of capitalism are parried by discussion of political freedom, and concepts of economic alienation and of the commodity system replaced by attacks on party bureaucracy, the 'new class,' and the like" (4). These substitutions, however, are not gratuitous or motivated by politics or false consciousness: inequality and power do have sources outside the economic, in structures of status, prestige, and lifestyle or culture. One might, therefore, argue contra Jameson that the charge of displacement focuses attention inappropriately, thwarting attempts to bring together—or, alternatively, to hold in tension—the Weberian "cultural" and "political" and the Marxian "economic." For surely it is the case that the "expropriation of the worker" is not solely the consequence of capitalism, but also, as Weber argued, of bureaucratization and the increasing centralization of rational administrative control, which is, indeed, a seemingly inescapable feature of the modern world, whether socialist or capitalist.

Norbert Elias points out—and doubtless Weber would agree—that "what is considered 'rational' depends at any time on the structure of society" (*Court* 110). From the point of view of the bourgeois or the capitalist, of a class society generally, what is most *irrational* about the structure of precapitalist society is its stratification by status,[4] in which, as Weber observes, a claim to social esteem carries with it certain privileges and is rooted principally in "a specific *style of life*" (932, 935, 938). Concerned principally with status, precapitalist society focuses not on the production of goods in a competition for wealth, but on the "*consumption* of goods" in a competition for prestige: "every status society lives by conventions, which regulate the style of life, and hence creates economically irrational consumption patterns and fetters the free market through monopolistic appropriations and by curbing the individual's earning power" (Weber 937, 307).

Stratification by class and by status, then, suggest alternate, and often opposed, modes of life. Elias identifies attitudes toward the use of money as one, perhaps the crucial difference between them. In a class society, or say, for the bourgeoisie, success requires the individual or the family to "subordinate expenses to income" in order to save for future capital investment. In a status society, or say, for the aristocracy, success requires conspicuous and competitive displays of one's status through, for example, lavish spending on houses and staffs to run them, on prodigious quantities of food and drink, on sumptuous and extravagant clothing, and on recreation and entertainment: the individual or the family must "make its expenditure dependent not primarily on its income but on its status and rank" (*Court* 66–67, 285). Truly, as Lawrence Stone comments, it is difficult for us to comprehend such consumption, to understand how "a single individual with a quarter of a million pounds a year or more—which in [mid-twentieth-century terms] is the sort of income enjoyed by the greater noblemen of the sixteenth and seventeenth centuries— could contrive to spend it and not infrequently to run up huge debts into the bargain" (249). But such expense, such public display, however seemingly irrational to us, is an investment made in the interests of social rather than financial return: for the aristocrat, "ownership of capital was finally a means to an end. It was significant primarily as a condition for upholding a social 'reality', the centrepiece of which was distinction from the mass of people, status as members of a privileged class, and behaviour that stressed this distinction in all the situations of life, in short, nobility as a self-evident value" (Elias, *Court* 96).

Maintaining distance and distinction from the mass of people requires, as Weber explains, "a monopolization of ideal and material goods or opportunities" (935). In early modern Europe, any number of legal and traditional prerogatives combined to distinguish gentry from commons, including rights to bear arms or to wear certain types of clothes or to possess serfs and bondsmen.[5] Veblen points out that the "economic expression of their superior rank" is the prohibition—whether legal or normative—against the gentry's entering into most forms of what Weber calls "rational economic pursuit, and especially entrepreneurial activity" (Veblen, *Leisure* 1; Weber 936). Thus, in England, the gentleman is one "who can live idly and without manuall labor," as Sir Thomas Smith explains in his 1583 treatise, *De Republica Anglorum* (72). And in France, the nobility were legally prohibited from engaging in commerce (Elias, *Court* 69), which exemplifies, perhaps, Weber's more general conclusion that "some status groups, and usually the most influential, consider almost any kind of overt participation in economic acquisition as absolutely stigmatizing" (937).

Of course this is not to say that in feudal societies the nobility were utterly idle, but only that, as Veblen asserts, they engaged, when they did engage, in "certain employments to which a degree of honour attaches. Chief among the honourable employments in any feudal community is warfare; and priestly service is commonly second to warfare" (*Leisure* 1). It is also to say that a freedom from manual labor or work is what most distinguishes the aristocracy from the mass of people and sets the stage for its particular style of life. Yet in doing so, it also sets the stage for the deep financial troubles faced by many English aristocrats in the late sixteenth and early seventeenth century. Aristocratic lifestyles required expenditures of huge sums of money, but as M. L. Bush points out, aristocrats "stubbornly sought to make ends meet without having to participate in commercial activities" (74).

Compelled by social norms on the one hand to spend but not to work, and on the other hand to leave relatively undisturbed the customary rents of their tenant farmers, English aristocrats waded through inflationary times, financing their lifestyles by receiving favor from the monarch or by marrying well or by mortgaging—and sometimes losing—land to merchant-usurers. Not uncommonly, the requirement that aristocratic lifestyles emphasize both consumption and idleness resulted in financial ruin, as Shakespeare demonstrates in *Timon of Athens*. Like Lord Timon—or any number of gallants in Jacobean city comedy—aristocrats discovered that "the greatest of your having lacks a half / To pay your present debts" (II.ii.147–48).

In rebuffing the steward's "sermon" on prodigality, and in acknowledging the ruin his gift giving has bought, Timon summarizes in one sentence the tension I have been describing between aristocratic and bourgeois assumptions about economics: "Unwisely, not ignobly, have I given" (II.ii.178). Here Timon acknowledges his economic foolishness, but he remains confident that his investment will pay dividends appropriate to the assumptions of the status society in which he lives. He can turn for help to those of his rank, he assures his steward, and thus can see his debts as "blessings; for by these / Shall I try friends. You shall perceive how you / Mistake my fortunes; I am wealthy in my friends" (II.ii.186–88).

At this crucial moment in the play, Shakespeare underscores the assumption of solidarity and reciprocity among the nobility, which Timon had previously emphasized to the crowd of banqueting lords: "I have often wish'd myself poorer that I might come nearer to you. We are born to do benefits; and what better or properer can we call our own than the riches of our friends? O what a precious comfort 'tis to have so many like brothers commanding one another's fortunes" (I.ii.98–103). As this passage and others make clear, money for Timon is necessary but quite secondary to living well, to displaying through lavish consumption his status, his position relative to others: both giving money and getting it result from a kind of generalized circulation that is, over time, more or less equitable among a group of men. Financial crisis thus allows Timon to test his friends, but what he tests is not primarily their affective ties to him but his status and prestige among them: "Ne'er speak or think / That Timon's fortunes 'mong his friends can sink" (II.ii.234–35). Such a test, moreover, "does not betray an attachment to externals, but to what was vitally important to individual identity," for "without confirmation of one's prestige through behaviour, this prestige is nothing" (Elias, *Court* 101).

Sink Timon's fortunes do; all his friends deny him. They fail to reciprocate as "like brothers"; instead, like Lucullus, they ignobly but wisely determine "that this is no time to lend money, especially upon bare friendship, without security" (III.i.41–43). It is a scandalous situation, according to the first stranger, who witnesses Lucius's sniveling refusal of aid, but one that registers again the tension between aristocratic and bourgeois attitudes toward economics: what the first stranger infers from the disagreeable situation is that "Men must learn now with pity to dispense, / For policy sits above conscience" (III.ii.85–86), the conscience that requires the aristocrat to give bountifully to others.

Since I have just downplayed the significance of affect in Timon's relationships with his friends and will soon turn to a reading of the critical literature on *Timon,* this is perhaps an appropriate moment to register my difference from Coppélia Kahn's fine reading of the play, which yokes feminist psychoanalysis to new historicism and even to anthropological theory, specifically to work by Marcel Mauss on gift exchange. But in her detailed and nuanced discussion of the play's relationship to Jacobean gift-giving, Kahn seems to ignore what Mary Douglas sees as the central lesson in Mauss: that there is no such thing as a free gift (vii) or, as Mauss himself puts it, what seems to be voluntary gift-giving is "in the final analysis . . . strictly compulsory, on pain of private or public warfare" (5; L. Wilson 79). Thus, after invoking Mauss and citing a Maussian comment by Louis Montrose about early modern patronage, which is "a tacitly coercive and vitally interested process predicated on the fiction that it is free and disinterested" (42), Kahn insists nevertheless that one of the "conflicting registers of social exchange" in *Timon* is free and disinterested, that is, the "ethos of disinterested friendship and diffuse reciprocity among peers inherited from Cicero and Seneca" (48). Timon, she claims, "gave as a friend, and expects to borrow as a friend, but instead he is being treated like any other debtor bound not by the ties of friendship but by the conditions of a legal contract" (50).

I think Kahn insists on the nonfictionality of free and disinterested exchange—thus taking the legacy of Cicero and Seneca at face value—largely because she is wedded to the notion that in contrast to anthropology or history, psychoanalysis offers fundamental explanatory power:

> It is tempting . . . to see the congruence of unconscious fantasy with social practice in the play as suggesting a partial explanation for the baffling persistence of the Jacobean patronage system in the face of its sheer unworkability. One cannot but wonder at the capacity of Big Men and ordinary courtiers alike to spend far beyond their means, borrow heavily, then live in undiminished splendor while falling into enormous debt that they could never realistically hope to repay. It seems possible that the extreme dependency created by patronage, in which advancement or obscurity, prosperity or ruin, hung on the granting of a suit, could have reawakened anxieties stemming from infantile dependency on the mother who, it seems to the child, can give or take away all. (57)

Perhaps. Perhaps psychoanalysis—reawakened anxiety, fear of the mother— does account for these historical facts. But perhaps a structural socioeconomic explanation accounts for this seemingly irrational or "baffling" behavior, and can do so without essentializing human emotional responses or describing them anachronistically.

That is, men must adapt to changing circumstances; those who do not will be ruined, like Timon, and forsake society in misguided misanthropy. Such might be distilled from the first stranger's comment cited above—"Men must learn now with pity to dispense, / For policy sits above conscience"—and be offered as the germinal seed of Shakespeare's play, save for the fact that the playwright loads the play in Timon's favor. As J. W. Draper put it in 1934, Shakespeare "clearly expected his audience to sympathise with Timon" (20). Critics have wrestled with what Draper calls the play's "fundamental paradox"—that Timon is "a bankrupt wastrel whose downfall we are expected to lament" (21)—principally and logically enough by denying Draper's charge, accepting the play's assertions about Timon's nobility and especially about the pernicious effects of economic rationality, of a society infused by money and what any number of critics have called the acquisitive principle. As Maurice Charney explains in a recent annotated bibliography of the play, "there is general agreement that the world of Timon is corrupt and that Athens is a materialistic, money-grubbing city in which virtue is doomed to cynical betrayal" (309).[6]

It is not surprising, therefore, to find in H. J. Oliver's introduction to the Arden edition of *Timon*, first published in 1959, the suggestion that "those twentieth century critics who have brought to the play their knowledge of the Elizabethan 'background' have . . . sometimes been blinded by such knowledge—blinded to the facts of the play" (xliv). Oliver finds distasteful the arguments of Draper and of E. C. Pettet, who think *Timon* "a straightforward tract for the times" (Pettet 321), depicting "the social chaos consequent . . . upon the economic ruin of the nobility (Draper 28) and thus casting Shakespeare, like some of his creations, as "a backward-looking lover of the old order" (Pettet 332) who wishes his audiences to sympathize with a "bankrupt wastrel" (Draper 21). It is difficult to discern whether Oliver dislikes Draper's and Pettet's characterization of Shakespeare's politics in this play or just their sullying of Timon's character or both. In any event, Oliver clearly thinks Draper's and Pettet's economic and historical analyses have missed the point of Timon's nobility, a nobility that for Oliver, as for many other critics, transcends his stupidity about economics. For Oliver and the others, as for Timon himself, acting "unwisely" is acceptable—or at least excusable—as long as "nobility" is preserved.

My point—and that of Weber and Elias, among others—is that economic irrationality largely constitutes nobility as a social reality and defines social stratification by status.[7] Thus, to the aristocrat or to anyone invested in or sympathetic to seeing social power distributed and regulated by nonmarket mechanisms, say, for example by birth or education, Timon's unwise but noble giving is both understandable and legitimate, even admirable. He becomes the disillusioned philanthropist, cruelly destroyed by a society focused on self-interest. To the bourgeois or to anyone invested in or sympathetic to seeing social power distributed and regulated through markets, Timon's unwise but noble giving is foolish and reveals him to be what Draper calls him, a "bankrupt wastrel," not quite the kind of fellow one would wish to occupy an elite position within society. To the bourgeois, Timon is misguided, first a prodigal and finally a misanthrope, blaming others for what he has brought upon himself.

In positing two such different frames of reference from which to view the play's action, I both follow and underscore the play's historical specificity and the kinds of lessons Marx inferred from his reading of Timon's paean to gold:

> Thus much of this will make
> Black, white; foul, fair; wrong, right;
> Base, noble; old, young; coward, valiant.
> Ha, you gods! Why this? What this, you gods? Why, this
> Will lug your priests and servants from your sides,
> Pluck stout men's pillows from below their heads.
> This yellow slave
> Will knit and break religions, bless th'accurs'd,
> Make the hoar leprosy ador'd, place thieves,
> And give them title, knee and approbation
> With senators on the bench. This is it
> That makes the wappen'd widow wed again:
> She whom the spital-house and ulcerous sores
> Would cast the gorge at, this embalms and spices
> To th'April day again.
>
> (IV.iii.28–42)

According to Jacques Derrida, Marx "love[d] the words of this imprecation.
. . . of this immense malediction of malediction," and he appropriated those
words "with a kind of delight whose signs are unmistakable" (42–43, 42).
Unlike many contemporary critics who focus on what might be called the personal or moral failings of the well-to-do, such as their greed or self-interest or
mean-spiritedness, Marx follows Timon's analysis in emphasizing instead the
structurally transformative power of gold or money: not what money does to
the personalities of those who have it, for one can be greedy or self-interested
or mean-spirited about the exchange of cattle or pigs or women, but what
money allows those who have it to do within or to society. As Marx writes in
the *Economic and Philosophical Manuscripts* (1844), "that which I am unable to
do as a *man,* and of which therefore all my individual essential powers are incapable, I am able to do by means of *money*" (168). Money gives to the individual
something inconceivable in traditional, largely static, precapitalist societies: the
power to "overturn . . . and confound . . . all human and natural qualities," to
bring about "the fraternization of impossibilities," as Marx says (*Manuscripts*
168); or as Timon says, the power to make "Black, white; foul, fair; wrong, right;
/ Base, noble; old, young; coward, valiant" (ll. 29–30).

What Marx, following Timon, complains about is the social revolutionary
force of capital, its potential to transform society structurally, to turn everything "into its *contrary*" (*Manuscripts* 168). Money, capital, is "a radical lev-

eller" that "extinguishes all distinctions" (*Capital* 229); money enables, as Derrida notes, a "transfiguring alchemy" (43). A thief's money puts him alongside senators on the bench, and the wappened widow's money brings her "to th'April day again." Money can buy blessing for the "accurs'd and / Make the hoar leprosy ador'd." Because money allows "social power [to become] the private power of private persons" (*Capital* 230), money disrupts and eventually destroys traditional, hierarchical social orders. Timon rails and rants in the woods outside Athens because he has been forced to confront the deeply transformative, and no doubt in his eyes, the deeply corrosive and evil effects of rationalized economic behavior.

In *Timon of Athens*, Shakespeare prompts us, as Marx saw, to think about a specific historical moment, about how the development of a rationalized economy transforms a society structurally—disturbing old certainties, undermining old hierarchies, and, according to Derrida, confusing "in equivalency the proper and the improper, credit and discredit, faith and lie, the 'true and the false,' oath, perjury, and abjuration" (44). Or, as Marx says, Shakespeare prompts us to think about how a rationalized economy turns everything into its opposite, including, in this particular instance, the soul of bounty into a self-exile, a misanthrope. Marx would like us to agree that what happens to Timon is predictive or symbolic of what will happen to society under the influence of money and capital. But making this argumentative leap depends partly upon an idealization of what Timon was, of his liberality and generosity; it depends upon an idealization of the old order of feudalism, of economic irrationality, and of stratification by status.

This is a leap almost all critics of *Timon* make, a leap justified by Shakespeare's construction of the play around "a critique of money and money-oriented economies," as Michael Chorost, one of *Timon*'s recent critics, puts it (349). My argument with this position is not that critics are wrong about the play's critique of rationalized economics. In fact, if *Timon* does what Draper and Pettet think it does, presenting the cold hard facts of early-seventeenth-century economic life while casting Timon himself as a sympathetic, even tragic, character, then Shakespeare must build the play around such a critique. Rather, what I question in critical opinion about the play is the readiness, the gusto with which critics embrace Shakespeare's "critique of money and money-oriented societies," a critique made in defense of an arguably parasitic, self-indulgent elite, whose dominance and pleasure resulted in and depended on the brutalization, the abject misery, of the masses of people.[8] It is as if the vast majority of *Timon*'s critics are beleaguered aristocrats, fearful of the disruptive, subversive, leveling power of money and markets, which as Timon laments can "bless th'accursed, / Make the hoar leprosy ador'd, place thieves, / And give them title, knee and approbation / With senators on the bench."

Earlier I pointed out that all societies are stratified, or ranked; inequality is, shall we say, in the nature of things. Capitalism, Fernand Braudel reminds us, "does not invent hierarchies, any more than it invented the market, or production, or consumption" (75). If inequality is a given, it might seem a bit of a toss-up as to which institutionalization of inequality is better—or worse. One might expect to be involved in both theoretical and empirical debates about the issue. Yet critics seem eager to assume that the inequality characteristic of precapitalist or preindustrial societies was or is better than the inequality characteristic of capitalist societies. This is not an argument, but a postulate, and one that is not restricted to contemporary materialist critics on the left.

Indeed, capitalism is routinely demonized in critical discourse.⁹ So pervasive is this demonization that Marjorie Perloff has called it a "pious cliché," one that is "repeated again and again in critical texts that claim to have no particular bias" (130). But as Bristol points out, such "sentiments are not of recent emergence"; scholars have long desired "to be counted as separate from and oppositional towards the imperatives of the market, commodity exchange, and industrial discipline" (*America* 35). Despite differences of pitch and moment, then, anticapitalism unites critics of the left and the right, as Hugh Grady suggests in pointing out the "limited but striking convergence of interests and ideas between the American New Critics and the Frankfurt School" (154). In the mid-1940s, John Crowe Ransom published Theodor Adorno's work in the *Kenyon Review* because he found much to agree with in his "Theses upon Art and Religion Today"; both Ransom and Adorno "found in art a possible weapon against the levelling and sterilizing processes of capitalist modernization, and both believed fiercely in the need to preserve art's autonomy, not in order to escape from social reality but in order to preserve the alternatives to it contained within the forms of art" (156).¹⁰

It does not surprise us, therefore, to read that "Marx . . . was a Shakespearian," or at least the kind of Shakespeare who writes *Timon of Athens* (Muir 57). Nor does it surprise us to read that Andrew Marvell's "Upon Appleton House" registers a revolutionary moment in the development of capitalist inequality, after which "there can be no question of returning to, or of salvaging the comparative humanity of, some previous settlement" (Kendrick 14). Whether "some previous settlement" offers "comparative humanity" to the people operating in the entire structure of production is debatable; but it is not debatable for Christopher Kendrick. I would argue, in contrast, that the "comparative humanity" of feudal production as opposed to capitalist production depends on whom you are concerned about. Let me concede, as indeed I already have, that capitalism involves a desocialization of labor. I concede, as Bauman argues, that what labor rebels against in the transition from feudal to capitalist society and in the development of its class consciousness is not the extraction of surplus value, or even its management and distribution, but capitalism's assault "on the autonomy of the producer" (18). Under the "previous settlement," laborers were left alone to produce because "the old power was geared to the task of creaming off the surplus product; it was never confronted, at least on an important scale or for prolonged periods, with the need to organise the production itself" (Bauman 46).

Let me concede, then, that the tenant farmer in 1500 wielded more autonomy in his production than does the computer assembler in 2000. But by any *material* standard—income, disposable income, education, housing, life expectancy, and so on—the computer assembler is vastly better off than the tenant farmer. "Autonomy" versus "material well-being": such a trade-off, if indeed it is one, is not to be countenanced by the professional literary critic. For us, autonomy is a principle virtue and goal,[11] not to be despoiled by materialism and never to be sacrificed merely for material gain, which is why Fish can take "the relationship between academics and their Volvos . . . [as] emblematic of a basic academic practice, the practice of translating into the language of higher motives desires and satisfactions one is unable or unwilling to acknowledge." Putting "the matter in the form of a rule or rule of thumb," Fish concludes: "whenever you either want something or get something, manage it in such a way as to deny or disguise its material pleasures" ("Volvos" 103).

Other people, people who labor, for instance, may be less inclined than critics to "deny . . . material pleasures"—a tract home, with built-in appliances; a powerboat; a dirt bike; three, four, even five TVs; video games; fast food; cases of cheap beer. Yet critics deny not only our own material pleasures, which—let us be plain—are numerous, but also those of people who have few other pleasures, as, for example, books, art, or the life of the mind. We insist that they focus on their alienation from the means of production and regale them with lectures that their pleasures, the stuff they buy with the wages of their alienation, are measures of their oppression or co-optation; their failure, not their success. We refuse to consider that exchanging (some) autonomy on the job for material pleasures is, or at least might be, a reasonable choice. As Carolyn Kay Steedman observes in her working-class autobiography *Landscape for a Good Woman,* "within the framework of conventional political understanding, the desire for a New Look skirt cannot be seen as a political want, let alone a proper one" (121).

Fish thinks that academics' disdain for stuff is *purposeful*, since this "disdain . . . is itself a sign of a dedication to higher, if invisible, values" ("Volvos" 104, 105). Writers from working-class backgrounds, such as Steedman or Gloria Anzaldúa, think that the disdain of material well-being characteristic of academic radicalism is born of privilege and reflects (upper) middle-class bias. But we can identify another purpose and another bias: prejudging the issue of inequality and romanticizing feudalism—the obsession with alienation and the stubborn unwillingness, via the demonization of stuff, even to consider that capitalism is an effective way to better the material life of people—reveals our concern to be principally with ourselves, our lifestyles, and our values. To the extent that they threaten (intellectual) autonomy, alienation and consumerism threaten us, and thus we project our anxiety about modes of capitalist production onto the working class. We fight capitalism not in our own name, not in our own interests, but selflessly, in the interests of the oppressed.

Such projection is true even of discussions of intellectual autonomy and labor that differentiate among segments of intellectual labor and that focus on and even openly promote the protection of intellectuals' own interests, such as Guillory's "Literary Critics as Intellectuals." Guillory concludes that the protection of our interests depends "especially upon promoting the recognition that intellectual autonomy—and therefore intellectuality—is always potentially at stake in work autonomy, which is at stake in every sector of intellectual labor, and of labor in general" (141). Guillory cannot resist this gesture—the sentence must allow "intellectuality" to trickle down, finally, to "labor in general"—despite his own admission much earlier in the essay that it is possible to posit "a constitutive distinction between intellectual and manual labor, a distinction that for good historical reasons implicates intellectual labor in the system of economic exploitation" (110). Given that socioeconomic reality, that responsibility for economic exploitation, Guillory wonders "how the fact of intellectual labor becomes the condition for the innate tendency to progressive or even leftist politics that is assumed to characterize intellectuals" (110–11). A good question is deferred indefinitely by turning immediately—in the next sentence—to "the discourse of intellectuals *about themselves*," a constraint that allows intellectuals to be defined "as a political and not a socioeconomic identity" (111), thus clearing away that "constitutive distinction" and preparing the stage for his final return to an intellectual labor that rather than exploitative is liberating, a good to be desired and fought for "in . . . every sector of . . . labor in general" (141).

This is misrecognition on a large scale. I contend that the profession's anticapitalism, and perhaps especially its obsession with alienation and autonomy, is consistent with our self-interest and not necessarily with any other group's self-interest. As professionals working in educational institutions, we constitute a powerful status group, not unlike early modern aristocrats, competing more for prestige—for "honor and reputation," according to Thomas L. Haskell (219)—than for money. Fish concurs, noting that we compete for "attention, applause, fame, and ultimately, adulation of a kind usually reserved for the icons of popular culture" ("Volvos" 103). And whether or not we acknowledge it consciously, our status as a status group largely affects our socioeconomic identity (and hence, I would add in contrast to Guillory, our political identity): as argued in chapter 2, it is in our professional interests to oppose (full) democratic access to knowledge, and as argued here, it is in our professional interests to oppose the development of market economies and certainly of market sensibilities within our profession. Truly, as Brint admits, the professions are "neither democratic nor capitalist" (16).

Markets are highly subversive and volatile arenas, in which money—economic success, however achieved—speaks loudest about the distribution of privilege, as much or more so than birth or talent or intelligence. Those interested in preserving aristocratic or intellectual privilege do well to resist capitalist development because, in short, it gives the vulgar a voice, a voice they exercise in a market. As Weber remarks, a "status order would be threatened at its very root if mere economic acquisition and naked economic power still bearing the stigma of its extra-status origin could bestow upon anyone who has won them the same or even greater honor as the vested interests claim for themselves" (936). In the academy, "mere economic acquisition" will not do; a security guard, for example, cannot win the lottery, decide that she would like to teach Shakespeare, and buy the position. One becomes a professor by acquiring proper credentials after years and years of study, by proving oneself worthy in an arena vastly different from the economic; and today, artists or—even more tellingly, an entrepreneur—must usually possess the appropriate "terminal degree" to work in a university.

Nonmarket, and in many cases actively antimarket, values and behaviors have dogged the history of professions in the United States, and were especially prominent during the period 1860–1960, when what Brint calls "social trustee professionalism" dominated our understandings of what it meant to be a professional (37). In tracing the history of modern professions, Larson identifies from the beginning a "fusion of antithetical ideological structures and a potential for permanent tension," since a necessary ingredient in organizing for success *within* a market was the assertion and incorporation of nonmarket tendencies, of "ideological supports connected with 'anti-market' structures of stratification" (*Rise* 63; Brint 5–8, 15–17, 36–39). That is, as nineteenth-century physicians and lawyers organized themselves as professionals, they latched onto norms associated with preindustrial social formations, such as gentility, disinterestedness, noblesse oblige, ritualization, even sacralization, all of which helped to establish the quality of the services being offered on the market. At the same time, however, the professions' embrace of these norms "reinforced the ideological persistence of 'old' stratification structures" (Larson, *Rise* 66). Or, as Bledstein puts it, professionalization "had only socially conservative consequences," as it "cultivated the inner aristocratic or elitist social instincts" of the emergent professionals (92, 93).

Decrying the (recent or increasing) intrusion of market values and behavior into the professions is potentially disingenuous on at least two fronts. First, it promotes a nostalgic vision that professionals once were disinterested, and should again "subordinate self-interest to higher ends—the truth, the public interest, the welfare of individual clients, the quality of the work itself—and thereby stand on a higher moral plane than those who merely truck and trade in the marketplace" (Haskell 181). We know that such an image of professionalism never was accurate, and, as Haskell points out, for the most part nowadays "reactions to it range from mild skepticism to curt dismissal" (181).

Second, and more importantly, it attempts to displace entirely onto capitalism responsibility for what Krause calls the "death of the guilds," of professional power. Krause himself accepts that both the state and capitalism are rivals of the professions, and both Brint and Krause recognize that through legislation, such as antidiscrimination laws, and court decisions, such as those allowing advertising and competitive bidding among professionals, the state contributed significantly to the breakdown of professional power. Indeed, and although I would say both Brint and Krause downplay this relationship, it is arguable that the infusion of market values and behavior into the professions results to a large extent from what Brint calls "demographic change" in the professions since 1970, the democratization of access to the professions resulting in massive increases in the numbers of professionals generally and of women and minorities in particular (cf. Krause 29–78). Quite simply, stiff competition in the professional marketplace—today more than twice as many doctors and lawyers and academics practice in the United States than did in the 1960s—has eroded professionals' antimarket sensibilities, their attachment to the "cultural ideals of the old aristocracy" (Brint 8), and has reoriented their attention toward the development of marketable expertise and the pursuit of their own pecuniary interests. It is difficult to resist the conclusion that for the professions at least, democratization and the infusion of market values and behavior go hand in hand, that democratization cannot be achieved without undermining what was a sheltered market position. And thus it is difficult to resist the conclusion that concern over professionals' loss of economic exclusivity masks concern for another loss, one that nowadays cannot be named— the loss of social exclusivity.

"Social trustee" professionalism has been debunked, its status as, in Brint's terms, a "functional aristocracy," neither democratic nor capitalist, exposed (63). As literary critics, however, we have a second reason to oppose the market, since unlike, say, engineers or accountants and other business-friendly practitioners of what Brint calls "expert professionalism," the market threatens us over issues of our area of professional expertise: judgment and value. To this point I turn in the next chapter. For now, it shall suffice, I hope, to observe that a number of scholars now agree that the Romantic aesthetic, the aesthetic of disinterest, which governs literary judgment to this day, flowers in response to pressure from the developing literary marketplace, a market that, like all markets, allowed the vulgar a voice in the determination of value. Anticapitalism among writers and academics is clearly bound up with antipopulism, with a need to keep the masses at bay and to delegitimate their voices, their judgments. To the extent that antipopulism is a subtext of anticapitalism, the mystification inherent in upper-middle-class academics' trumpeting of the virtues of precapitalist economics and social organization is intensified.

By way of conclusion, let me say again that understanding stratification in early modern England is difficult and problematic. How could it be otherwise? Not only is this a period of class formation but also one during which class begins to emerge as a principle of stratification and as a concept. And despite the problematization of almost everything in our discourse, we literary critics have only begun to problematize "class" and have yet to problematize "capitalism." Perhaps this theoretical slackness results from our having given our allegiance for the most part to a theoretical framework that assigns class and capitalism a negative moral value, thus absolving us of obligations to complicate our understandings of them. Or perhaps more generally it results from a lack of imagination endemic to interdisciplinary work in literary study: many of us turn immediately to those working in the traditions of Marx and Freud, and thus need not even demonize competitors working in the traditions of Weber or Emile Durkheim or William James, because only what is acknowledged to exist can be demonized.

I give much credit to that functional or institutional argument because I know well the allure of lines of least resistance. But our failure to distinguish between class and status as concepts, as modes of stratification with differing systems of meanings, results, I propose, from the power of our own contemporary political allegiances, including an unwillingness to confront our own awkward relationship to capitalism and the people and an unwillingness, more generally, to confront the seriousness of the Weberian challenge to Marx and the Marxian tradition. For it is a serious challenge indeed: confronting Weber and confronting the meanings of inequality rooted in status differentiation means confronting ourselves and the ideology, rooted in the Marxian tradition, by which, whether partially or fully, a lot of us order our lives as privileged intellectuals. And ideology, as James H. Kavanagh reminds us, *is* a "system of representations that offer[s] the subject an imaginary, compelling, sense of reality in which crucial contradictions of self and social order appear resolved" (145).

CHAPTER FOUR

Fobbing Off Disgrace with a Tale
Stories about Voices in *Coriolanus*

I was three, maybe four years old. My elderly mother couldn't quite remember that detail or, for that matter, what time it was; but it was late, late for cooking dinner. My sense is that it might have been nine o'clock or even somewhat later. What Mom did remember was the doctor's anger at being stirred from his home and his rapidly shrinking evening to meet us at the emergency room. "What was she doing up so late?" he demanded, after examining my badly burned foot. "Why on earth wasn't that little girl in bed?"

Unlike Ursula in Jonson's *Bartholomew Fair*, Mom was scolded, too, for slathering my foot in margarine after the accident happened, after I got my foot in the way of the can she was pouring grease into, boiling grease in which she was making freshly cut french fries for my dad's dinner. Did I trip her, get caught up in her housedress or feet? Or was I scurrying on the countertops, as I often did, especially when she or my dad wasn't looking, undisciplined and quick as a cat? I don't know, and Mom couldn't remember, but something slipped in an instant and the hot grease hurt like nothing I'd ever felt. My foot bubbled, looking like the plastic packing wrap that was not yet invented. Dad leapt from his chair, where he was drinking beer and smoking cigarettes and watching television, to help Mom try to calm me down; and we shot off to the hospital, where we learned from the doctor, "It's ice, not fat, for burns." The fat just kept the foot frying, so to speak, making it worse.

Such a story, you might think, is not one that would have lived for my mom, taking a place in her repertoire alongside tales of being left to die at birth; or orphaned at seven; or married at sixteen, thirty, and thirty-eight (producing three children in the first marriage, two in the second, and one, me, in the third); or chasing away, with broom or pocketbook, the predatory females her husbands attracted. (Not to suggest that she herself did not attract a number of predatory males; she did.) But, like the story of having to fight school administrators to prevent my sister from being held back or the story of watching the police brutalize a possibly vagrant, probably unemployed, and decidedly harmless Euro-American man who had lingered one night in the street in front of our house, the story of my foot was told often enough, and only recently have I been able to make a story to account for it and others of its kind.

The story I want to tell is this: beneath a fierce desire to enable her children to live a better and easier life than she had led, a desire that required her to promote behavior that would lead to upward mobility, lay two frightening and related recognitions. The first, as argued in chapter 2, is that encouraging upward mobility entails the high probability of losing your child, sometimes literally and usually figuratively. The second is that the kinds of people she wanted her children to be—members, say, of what would soon be called the New or professional-managerial class—were not the kind of people she trusted or believed or liked. And perhaps more importantly, Mom knew that, in general, they were not the kind of people who liked her: "professionals," report Derber, Schwartz, and Magrass, "feel farthest removed from working people" and share a "crude view of the culture of workers" (158; Lasch 28–29). Truly, as Barbara and John Ehrenreich observe, the relationship between the professional middle class and the working class is "objectively antagonistic" (17).

Mom's stories operated simultaneously on several not necessarily mutually reinforcing levels. Cautionary tales told us what not to do: not to leave school, not to get married at sixteen, not to let your husband dominate you if you did. Other tales, tales of fortitude and strength, suggested that fate and even mistakes and bad decisions should be overcome. But the story of my foot and others like it worked differently, to undercut the imperative to succeed, to assure us that value and worth ultimately reside elsewhere than in status or income. Professionals, these stories implied, don't know everything, even about their own business—what exactly is the harm in a four-year-old staying up until ten o'clock anyway?—and yet they try to overwhelm and humiliate the working person who is at a disadvantage because of education, prestige, and income. Mom knew that the professions' "service ideal" is precisely that, an ideal, and that it works more often in the real world as ideological justification for privilege and domination. Like Shakespeare's Timon, she knew that "there is boundless theft / In limited professions" (*Timon* IV.iii.430–31).

Although like most working-class people, Mom experienced "the PMC primarily in their regulatory roles as teachers, bosses, and 'expert' professionals" (Croteau 41), she nevertheless would have given credit to Bruce Robbins's apologia for professionals and the service ideal. She thought well of people and would have accepted his argument that "just because you are looking for trouble does not mean there is not trouble there to be found—and it may mean that you will have the chance to do something about it" ("Theory" 8). She would have conceded, I think, Robbins's point that "professional independence" is not in every instance "won . . . by reducing nonprofessionals to dependence" ("Theory" 8). (After all, such an assertion cannot be disproved.) But she would also have hoped—and argued—that Robbins acknowledge more fully, more imaginatively perhaps, that in *most* cases dependency for the mass *is* the cost of professional independence for the few. It is not just that professionals routinely engage in "intellectual imperialism," extending "claims of specialized knowledge promiscuously" and thus "inappropriately diminishing clients'" (Derber, Schwartz, and Magrass 150). It is also that, as Bledstein concludes, the "very idealism . . . of professionalism [breeds] public attitudes of submission and passivity," attitudes of such strength and surety that "no metaphysical authority more effectively humbled the average person" (104, 105).[1]

The humbling of the average person is my subject in this chapter and the next. Previous chapters have unpacked at least part of this domination, arguing that the demonization of capital functions in part to mystify the power of knowledge to impose hierarchy and inequality. Intellectuals' anticapitalism, therefore, is an "interested" opposition. To begin this chapter, I wish to develop further this interested opposition to capitalism: to argue that the subtext—or perhaps, the bottom line—of intellectuals' anticapitalism is antipopulism, a fear of the people and their voices. We oppose capitalism in the name of the people but do so to protect our own prerogative of judgment over them in the marketplaces for culture.

Capitalism is, of course, vulgar. As mentioned in chapter 3, what distinguishes the nobility, the gentry, and the well-educated from the mass of people in early modern Europe is freedom from engaging in trade, commerce, or physical labor. As argued there, those interested in preserving professional, intellectual, or aristocratic privilege do well to resist capitalist development, for markets are highly subversive and volatile arenas, in which money, regardless of how it is obtained—whether "by sweaty effort or by cheating or perhaps by plain luck," as Berger playfully observes (53)—is what counts in the distribution of privilege, as much as or more than birth or talent or intelligence. Capitalism allows the vulgar a voice, a voice they exercise in the market, which, when played very successfully, can then be exercised elsewhere, as in universities or the halls of government.

The preceding sentence, I realize, suggests that casting a vote in the marketplace is more effective in giving the vulgar a voice within society than either mass education or the widening of the franchise within representative democracy. I make this claim because, as argued in chapter 2, formal and higher education offers the vulgar voice, but principally upon the condition of assimilation into the (upper) middle class, a condition that clearly works to minimize and regulate that voice. Representative democracy also works to minimize and regulate the effect of the citizen's voice through institutions such as separate legislative houses, independent judicial branches, and electoral colleges, not to mention its historical restrictions on the franchise. In a society in which year by year representatives represent more and more people, this effect (or intent) only becomes more obvious. In the United States—and I shall repeat this claim somewhat differently in discussing *Coriolanus* below—the majority does not rule, and for this, many people are happy. As Benjamin Barber argues, elites tend to agree that "the more invidious pathologies of our grim era have derived from democratic excess," from participation, as if "popular government carries within itself a seed of totalitarian despotism" that can only be resisted through regimes of reason and social control (93, 94).

Equally effective in humbling the average citizen is the professionalization of politics, the infusion into politics of the elitist formations of education (Croteau 148–68; Derber, Schwartz, and Magrass 206–10), which Bledstein recognizes in the progressive reforms of the late nineteenth century (104) and which a host of others recognize in the procedural reforms of the Democratic Party after the debacle of the 1968 national convention (Aronowitz, *Death;* D. Carter; Croteau; Diggins; Edsall; Edsall and Edsall; Gitlin, *Dream;* Lasch; MacInnes; Sleeper; Tomasky). Intended to open the political process by reducing the influence of then current party machinery and bosses, reform in both instances resulted mainly in the transfer of power to a different elite—in the case of the Democrats in the 1970s, to a better educated and wealthier elite, who have far less personal contact with and far less interest in the lives of the vast majority of voting citizens than did the operators of political machines. Concludes worker J. R. Hammond, who "by accident" became a delegate to the Democratic National Convention in 1992: one of the problems "with the American political process" is that the people are not "regulars" within the Democratic Party (157, 153).

In terms of policy, the result of transferring power to the well-to-do and highly educated has been a Democratic Party more roundly conservative on economic issues, which in 1978 anticipated regressive Reaganesque tax policy,[2] and more brazenly liberal on social and cultural issues—orientations that are precisely opposite to those of the working class (Brint 14, 19, 80, 86–87, 103, 117–18, 178; Croteau; Derber, Schwartz, and Magrass; Gitlin, *Dream*). In terms of participation, evidence reveals a sharp decline in voting among the poor and working class relative to the affluent (Edsall 179–201; Lasch 112–44; Gitlin, *Dream* 234), which leads Croteau to conclude that while middle-class people "engage in politics . . . working people survive it" (170). Or as Barber puts it, politics is "something done . . . to . . . citizens" (133).

Participation in both education and politics is not open or democratic but highly selective, the result of a winnowing process that leaves most people in the dust. But even the dustiest folks can buy and sell, as Ben Jonson makes clear in *Bartholomew Fair*. Even the dustiest folks, like Jonson's hobbyhorseman or pigwoman, participate in an exchange process that, as Peter Stallybrass and Allon White argue, was and is an "agent of transformation" (36), of enlargement and empowerment, both for the individuals engaged in it and for the community as a whole:

> Part of the transgressive excitement of the fair for the subordinate classes was *not* its "otherness" to official discourse, but rather the disruption of provincial habits and local tradition by the introduction of a certain cosmopolitanism, arousing desires and excitements for exotic and strange commodities. . . . Whilst this process might well present itself to the bourgeois bystander as the elevation or corruption of the rustic, to the villager it may well have been a more complex process—a form of defamiliarization in which the romantic-commercial novelty of foreign commodities confronted and relativized local custom. Nostalgia for the "truly" local and communal was undoubtedly more prevalent amongst the élite than amongst those who, at the fair, had a rare opportunity to admire and try on the customs of the world. (37)

Such nostalgia is common among contemporary elites as well; it does not require much imagination to construct (upper) middle-class responses to the prospect of Avon calling at the riverside dwellings of Brazilian Indians or of a Wal-Mart superstore lighting up the night sky in Vermont. But for the Indian women, in Brazil or elsewhere, as for the villagers going to the fair in early modern England or for working-class people in the United States today, the prospect of a "certain cosmopolitanism," purchased even at a very high price, is not exclusively or necessarily exploitative or destructive of local or traditional life. Despite the protestations of Zeal-of-the-Land Busy or his contemporary inheritors, it is neither evil nor wrong to want what you lack.

Capitalism, as Tawney points out, is "intent on the widening of opportunities rather than the maintenance of privileges" (*Usury* 135).[3] What *do* you lack? Notice that in Jonson's play, "the religious censor, Busy, the educational censor, Wasp, and the state censor, Overdo, are taken away to be put in the stocks" from just outside Ursula the pigwoman's booth (Stallybrass and White 65). Ursula's booth is indeed symbolically significant in this instance, as the disruption if not overthrow of privilege in *Bartholomew Fair* is presented as benign and even healthy: Overdo is humbled in his quest to ferret out "enormities" and reign in excess.

Yet it is clear that *Bartholomew Fair*'s celebration of the market is neither unambiguous nor representative of elite attitudes or even of Jonson's. On the one hand, contemporary scholarship now resists modernist assertions, such as those of L. C. Knights, that Jonson routinely attacks capitalist acquisitiveness. In rewriting Knights's *Drama and Society in the Age of Jonson,* Don Wayne suggests that Jonson's work and *Bartholomew Fair* in particular is implicated in the production and promulgation of "the emergent ideologies associated with capitalist development in England" (27)—such as individualism, rational self-interest, and the notion of a social contract.[4] On the other hand, the play is, as Jonas Barish observed years ago, "more radical than its author" (235). And in it, Jonson nicely registers the anxiety produced for playwrights by the demands of the market, imagining, to cite just one example, a contract with his audience in which each member may have a "free-will of censure, to like or dislike," but only according to how much each has paid: "marry, if he drop but sixpence at the door, and will censure a crown's worth, it is thought there is no conscience or justice in that" (Ind. 92–93, 101–3).

Stallybrass and White explain Jonson's attempts to reduce that anxiety, arguing that he sought to

> stabilize and dignify an emergent place for authorship at a distance both from the aristocracy and the plebeians, and yet this authorial investiture— for that is what it aspired to be—was only locatable, "groundable", through its symbolic relation to existing hierarchies, existing languages, symbols and practices of high and low. The insertion of professional authorship *between* these was a fraught negotiation of a "middle" space and a complex contestation of traditional dichotomies. Authorship in this sense required a two-handed fending off of royal and popular patronage alike, since both entangled the poet in symbolic arrangements, rituals and deferences which no longer quite answered his *professional* needs. (74–75; 66–79; Loewenstein)

It is perhaps for reasons such as these that the play came to hold an anomalous position within Jonson's work, excluded not only by Knights from among Jonson's best but also by Jonson from the 1616 folio, excluded in the latter case for unexplained reasons, but quite likely because the "pig-wallow"—as Stallybrass and White, following Edmund Wilson, tag the play—undermines the strategies of professionalization and literary elevation of which the folio *Workes* was a part.

Jonson is not the only playwright among England's first group of professionals to register anxiety about his relationship to paying customers: in the metatheatrical *The Knight of the Burning Pestle,* Francis Beaumont dramatizes the playwright's nightmare, a citizen-grocer who emerges from the audience to undertake a redirection of the play, to fashion it "in honor of the commons of the city" (Ind. 27–28). More famously, in *Hamlet,* Shakespeare's prince advises the players to attend in their performances to the requirements of the "judicious" few, whose judgment "must . . . o'erweigh a whole theatre of others'," the "groundlings, who, for the most part, are capable of nothing but inexplicable dumb shows and noise" (III.ii.26, 27–28, 11–12). Examples of this anxiety abound in the period, though I have only cited a few, and it is possible, therefore, to hypothesize an ambivalence in writers' and artists' relationships to the developing market economy of the seventeenth century, an ambivalence that, as a literary marketplace establishes itself in the eighteenth century, develops into hardened opposition determined to "stem the commercialization of literature" and to disarticulate a work's value from its popularity (Woodmansee 4, 78). It was a situation in which "the free play of genius found it increasingly difficult to consort with the free play of the market" (Williams, *Culture* 47). Therefore, and in a move similar to the moves made in response to the market by emerging professionals, which I discussed in the previous chapter, the Romantics and their Victorian successors refused either to submit to the market's tyranny or to oppose its workings in general. Instead, according to Jean-Christophe Agnew, they "merely consented to operate outside its dominion. Aestheticism and economism effectively cartelized the social world by dividing cultural exchange and market exchange into separate disciplinary jurisdictions" (6–7).[5]

As with professionalism, it is easy to locate in this move romanticism's "constitutive hypocrisy," as Eric Gans puts it, the fact that "the romantic, whether of the right or of the left . . . is in principle hostile to the market. But the romantic lifestyle, with the predictable exception of the few radicals, suicides, and the like who took its precepts too literally, is in fact a preparation for life and career in market society" (166). Still, and again as with professionalism, one has to admit that it was an effective maneuver. And it still dominates our thinking about art and commerce. Even Charlie the Tuna, spokesfish for the

Starkist Company, knows that "good taste" excludes a tuna from the fate of tuna that "taste good"—to be absorbed "into the apparatus of production and consumption," or, less abstractly, "to be butchered, cooked, and canned" (Bristol, *America* 15–16).

Much in the projects of Woodmansee, Lawrence Levine, and John Carey aims to point out the self-interest and the elitism of such cartelizing. Woodmansee is quite frank about this: Schiller, for example, was unable to produce new work in a timely manner (4, 79–80) and Coleridge, although aware of what his readers required, actively resisted "accommodating them, even his most privileged readers—the doctors, lawyers, lords, professors, clergymen, and landowners who constituted the intended audience of his ill-fated periodical of 1809–10, *The Friend*" (143). Like other serious writers of the time, Schiller and Coleridge found it preferable to deride their audiences than to adjust their work habits or writing styles to the market. Since the reading public did not buy what the serious writers offered, what the reading public did buy was redefined by them as unworthy. Failed reception, therefore, indicated not "an imperfect work, but . . . the imperfect sensibility . . . of the audience" (21).

A flight from the market and the people can be documented in America, as well. Like Woodmansee, Levine is frank about the conjoining of interests in the development of American cultural institutions, including educational institutions, a conjoining that in the late nineteenth century led away from the market, away "from the mixed audience and from the presence of other cultural genres" (230).[6] Not able to find adequate financial support at the box office for the "pure" programs they wanted to produce, directors of symphonies, museums, and theaters increasingly looked to free themselves from what Paul DiMaggio calls "the grip of the marketplace (which ordinarily drives entrepreneurs to elide aesthetic distinctions in order to create larger audiences and discourages canon formation by providing incentives for presenters to differentiate their products)" (43–44). But at the turn of the century, since there was no patronage to be had from royalty or government, a move away from the market, from, shall we say, grassroots capitalism and the cultural choices of the people, meant on the one hand a move toward "paternalistic capitalism" (Levine 131–32)—the pocketbooks and the cultural preferences of a Vanderbilt, a Huntington, a Flagler—and on the other, a move toward "the universities, which in the United States have been the dominant centers in which cultural authority has been institutionalized, as well as the organizations most responsible for engaging the interest of young people in elite culture" (DiMaggio 44).

But then, it is the aim of this chapter to suggest that, *Bartholomew Fair* notwithstanding, elites tend to perceive the widening of opportunity, increasing the number and diversity of voices in marketplaces of culture, as risky business. Giving ground or opening the gates runs the risk of elites having to ante up to maintain distinction and distance, at considerable cost to themselves, as both Woodmansee and Carey show. Woodmansee, for example, points to the choices being made in the literary marketplace of the eighteenth century by a "new and rapidly expanding reading public" as motivating the "momentous shift from the instrumentalist theory of art to the modern theory of art as an autonomous object that is to be contemplated disinterestedly" (36, 32). A similar readjustment was found to be necessary about a century later, as modernist writers responded to the threat created by yet another large increase in the reading public. Huxley, Eliot, Forster, Woolf, Lawrence, Joyce, Pound, Orwell, and others "could not, of course, actually prevent the masses from attaining literacy. But they could prevent them from reading literature by making it too difficult for them to understand—and this is what they did. . . . [T]he principal around which modernist literature and culture fashioned themselves was the exclusion of the masses, the defeat of their power, the removal of their literacy, the denial of their humanity" (Carey 16, 21).

Coriolanus, literally and figuratively on his way to the marketplace—the liminal space, the boundaryless space—underscores the danger of giving ground, danger *Coriolanus*[7] records and examines and finally resolves—and resolves in a way that is amenable perhaps especially to intellectual elites. The Roman warrior warns:

> In soothing them, we nourish 'gainst our senate
> The cockle of rebellion, insolence, sedition,
> Which we ourselves have plough'd for, sow'd and scatter'd,
> By mingling them with us, the honour'd number
> Who lack not virtue, no, nor power, but that
> Which they have given to beggars.
>
> (III.i.68–73)

Implicit in Coriolanus's rages against the people—their cowardice, their dirty and callused hands, their fickle and inadequate minds, and so on—is that patrician culture is both distinct from and superior to that of the people, as Kenneth Burke pointed out years ago. Coriolanus, says Burke, "is *excessively* downright, forthright, outright (and even, after his fashion upright), in his unquestioned assumption that the common people are intrinsically inferior to the nobility ("Faction" 83).[8]

Explicit in Coriolanus's ragings is that the patricians have no one to blame but themselves for "mingling . . . the honour'd number" with the crowd, for blurring the distinction between them, and thus, for becoming dissolved in what is inferior, literally ignoble. Mingling with the crowd is dishonorable; it means to be debased by the crowd, overwhelmed by it, and even, perhaps, silenced by it:

> If you are learn'd
> Be not as common fools; if you are not,
> Let them have cushions by you. You are plebeians
> If they be senators; and they are no less
> When, both your voices blended, the great'st taste
> Most palates theirs.
>
> (III.i.98–103)

In that brew of voices, "the great'st taste / Most palates theirs," and the bad judgment of the multitude, if vocalized, will overwhelm the superior judgment of the elite, a potential disaster for both the aristocracy and the state. It is for this reason, reasons the warrior, that this voice must be silenced:

> Therefore beseech you—
> You that will be less fearful than discreet,
> That love the fundamental part of state
> More than you doubt the change on't; that prefer
> A noble life before a long, and wish
> To jump a body with a dangerous physic
> That's sure of death without it—at once pluck out
> The multitudinous tongue: let them not lick
> The sweet which is their poison.
>
> (III.i.148–56)

Coriolanus's outbursts here—recall that Menenius and the other senators repeatedly try to quiet him—suggest quite clearly that protecting (the prerogative of) judgment necessarily involves a policing of boundaries and the maintaining of distinction: "Your dishonour / Mangles true judgement, and bereaves the state / Of that integrity which should becom't" (ll. 156–58).

One might think that in these lines, the Roman warrior has got it backward, that bad judgment causes some form of dishonor, rather than the other way around. But dishonor does mangle true judgment for the nobility because it signifies the destruction of the conditions—the bounded conditions—under which judgment can be exercised. To lose one's honor, according to Elias, "was to forfeit membership of 'good society'" and thus to shatter the foundation of personal and social existence, "central to which was the maintenance of everything that traditionally held the lower-ranking strata at a distance, such things being of self-evident value to the aristocracy" (*Court* 95). To be dishonored—"By mingling them with us"—is to fail to maintain "distinction from the surrounding mass, without which [a noble's] life, as long as the power of privileged society remained intact, was meaningless" (Elias, *Court* 95). To be dishonored is to be cast outside the conditions of meaning, and therefore, as Coriolanus puts it, outside the conditions of "true judgement."

Mangle is a verb of violence and mutilation, appropriate in a play and for a society (not just Coriolanus's but also Shakespeare's) in which, as Stanley Cavell suggests, "speech is war" (167) and in which, as Elias argues, the courtier is the knight or, to put it historically rather than metaphorically, the knight is becoming the courtier. Cavell has written beautifully about this play, developing and expanding—and at times taking issue with—the insights of Janet Adelman's psychoanalytic reading. What I would like to do here is link both readings, and particularly Cavell's, to Elias's account of the civilizing process, thereby offering a somewhat more historicized reading than either Cavell's or Adelman's about what is going on in the play with respect to hierarchy and inequality in the body politic. I will then briefly contrast my reading with Annabel Patterson's recuperative reading of the play in *Shakespeare and the Popular Voice*.

According to Cavell and just about everyone else, this play is about the organization and maintenance of the body politic. Dominating criticism have been two approaches to this topic, the psychological and the political.[9] Perhaps reflecting his appreciation for Adelman's efforts, Cavell avers that the psychological approach has proved more fruitful, since "a political reading is apt to become fairly predictable once you know whose side the reader is taking, that of the patricians or that of the plebeians" (145). William Hazlitt, for one, might take exception to that assertion, but in any case, twenty pages later Cavell has partly disproved his own hypothesis, producing an unpredictable political reading of the play, which, rather than politics, emphasizes "the formation of the political, the founding of the city, . . . what it is that makes a rational animal fit for conversation, for civility" (165). Cavell's political reading does not focus on a predictable or repetitive taking of sides, the opposition of the privileged and the oppressed, the patricians and the plebeians, what Burke calls "the discriminatory motives intrinsic to society as we know it" ("Faction" 94). In discussing "the formation of the political," Cavell suggests a kind of historical moment, one that's neither unique nor always already here or there, and that places Coriolanus in opposition both to plebeians and to patricians, as society moves toward the "overcoming of narcissism, incestuousness, and cannibalism" (165) in the creation of itself as civil.

Coriolanus's problem—as well as Rome's and England's—is that he abhors the prospect of civil society, which, as Cavell and Adelman and Elias rightly note, requires the acknowledgment of dependence and hence, I argue, of negotiation and exchange (as opposed to independence and appropriation).[10] This situation accounts for the play's starkness, what Cavell calls the play's "famine of words," since a shared language exemplifies community (168, 165): words, like food and money, are what a community shares or circulates or exchanges. Burke claims that "Coriolanus throughout is respectful to the patricians and directs his insults only to the plebeians" ("Faction" 92–93), but Cavell hits closer to the mark in arguing that Coriolanus's "disgust by language" is not status-bound but sparked by all who speak: "it is irrelevant to Coriolanus whether the parable of the belly is interpreted with the patricians or with the plebeians as the belly, or as the tongue, or as any other part. What alarms him is simply being part, one member among others of the same organism" (169). To this extent, Shakespeare focuses in *Coriolanus* neither on inter- nor intrastatus conflict. Plebeians and patricians alike line up against Coriolanus in the formation of civil society.

Adelman wishes to see Coriolanus's predicament as universal and timeless: "We want him to acknowledge dependence, to become one of us; but at the same time we do not want to see him give in, because to do so is to force us to give up our own fantasy of omnipotence and independence. . . . Coriolanus has throughout given free expression to *our* desire to be independent, and we delight in his claim" (119–20, 119). Adelman can assert the universality of this desire and delight because, as Stephen Greenblatt might say, she does not historicize the psychological categories she invokes ("Psychoanalysis"). Moreover, as I have argued elsewhere, such a failure is a sign not just of an odd commitment to the social sciences' brand of universalism; it also suggests misrecognition of the protocols of scientific work, of the limits of scientific discourse ("Freeloading"). In contrast, and like Elias and Greenblatt, I see Coriolanus's predicament as historically specific and constrained. Additionally, however, I would argue that such a predicament is bounded both diachronically and synchronically.

It is not just that Coriolanus's assertions of independence and omnipotence set the stage for a world in which such assertions are construed as neurotic fantasies that we all indulge to some degree or another, as both Greenblatt and Elias suggest.[11] Rather and in addition, Coriolanus's assertions of independence and omnipotence "delight" some people and not others within a given historical moment; and even across time, some groups of people will never delight in Coriolanus. Shakespeare's plebeians do not delight, and neither do I: for the working class or the poor or the marginalized there is in him no fantasy, no memory, no trace of our independence, since to indulge such a fantasy or trace requires a level of relative independence that most people in most historical moments do not share. Coriolanus expresses nostalgia or fantasy for those in any historical moment who possess considerable social power, and in the early seventeenth century, the socially powerful might clearly recall the untrammeled independence and omnipotence of the medieval knight, a violent and vicious power that, in somewhat muted form, persists into their day. For others, like the plebeians, Coriolanus expresses little but horror or fear.

The plebeians have good reason to be afraid of Coriolanus; their fear is not simply a sign of their personal cowardice and hence of their lack of desert (cf. III.i.118–26). Their fear, like Coriolanus's freely expressed and absolute contempt for them, is a logical psychological result of the structure of warrior society, a society in which, according to Bristol, "the fundamental *raison d'etre* of social life is the state of affairs known as war. . . . This condition is not thought of as a 'necessary evil,' or even as the means toward some end such as, let's say, peace: it is, on the contrary, an end in itself, and in fact the only possible state of political well-being" ("Lenten" 210). This is a society that encourages a delight in violence, cruelty, and torture and that requires men to assert their dominance through personal physical skill—skill aided and abetted by some kind of monopoly on weaponry. It was, furthermore, a society in which self-restraint is weakly enforced, and people indulge their instincts and emotions "freely . . . directly . . . openly," resulting in social relations characterized by volatility and precariousness and, for most people, no doubt, fear and abjection (Elias, *Process* 164).

The plebeians are to Coriolanus as the butterfly is to his son, objects to be dominated or mutilated: "O' my word," says Valeria, "the father's son! . . . I saw him run after a gilded butterfly, and when he caught it, he let it go again, and after it again, and over and over he comes, and up again, catched it again; or whether his fall enraged him, or how 'twas, he did so set his teeth and tear it. Oh, I warrant how he mammocked it!" (I.iii.57, 60–65). Adelman notes in passing that this passage "seems more a comment on Coriolanus's childhood than on his fatherhood," as if young Martius appears in the play principally to reveal to us something about the origins of the grown man's cruelty (118). Adelman locates those origins in Coriolanus's fantasy of independence, his "forbidden wish to have power over his mother" (117); yet I wonder if young Martius does not rather remind us of the arduous and lengthy process of socialization to which the warrior submits, the process that focuses his life for battle and only for battle, which he will wage until he dies or for "as long as his strength permit[s], into old age" (Elias, *Process* 160). Young Martius reminds us of the process that molds the warrior: a boy's "confirmed countenance" in chasing butterflies becomes the "flower of warriors" who "before him . . . carries noise, and behind him . . . leaves tears. / Death that dark spirit, in's nervy arm doth lie, / Which, being advanc'd, declines, and then men die" (I.iii.59–60; I.vi.32; II.i.157–60).

Such socialization—by which the warrior seeks to achieve goals by physical combat and "the fury of his passion," acting principally upon impulse with little regard for the feelings or interests of others—is not anomalous or neurotic in the warrior societies of even the late Middle Ages. According to Elias, "wherever one opens the documents of this time, one finds the same: a life where the structure of affects was different from our own," where feelings and emotions are expressed more spontaneously and with less restraint (*Process* 483, 164, 176). Indeed, agrees Lawrence Stone, whereas "Englishmen of the educated classes today enjoy the reputation for unusual reserve and exceptional self-control under the most provoking circumstances," such was not the case "in the sixteenth and seventeenth centuries [when] tempers were short and weapons to hand. The behaviour of the propertied classes, like that of the poor, was characterized by the ferocity, childishness, and lack of self-control of the Homeric age" (108). By these lights, then, Coriolanus is not engaging in neurotic fantasy: his behavior is normal enough, so normal and so dangerous that the Tudors engaged throughout the sixteenth century in repeated efforts "to contain violence and bring it within tolerable limits," as Stone reminds us (113).

If Stone and Elias are correct about changes affecting the behavior of aristocrats in the sixteenth and seventeenth centuries, changes that moved them slowly from warrior to courtier (or litigant or entrepreneur), then it does not seem a stretch to see *Coriolanus* as documenting or even participating in that process of change. Whether the play expresses relief or reluctance at the transformation is doubtless undecidable and at this point possibly irrelevant (which is also true of Patterson's attempt to dislodge Victorian readings of *Coriolanus* by an appeal to the play's historical embeddedness; but more of that, later). What is pertinent for my purposes is not whether the play was or is inherently conservative or elitist (or not) but rather what the play suggests about the mechanisms of distinction and hierarchy, and, ultimately, how knowledge of those mechanisms is used, or not. We can get at the former by noting a few words of the warrior who, in answering the tribune of the people, confesses that "oft, / When blows have made me stay, I fled from words" (II.ii.71–72).

"I fled from words." Words frighten Coriolanus because they imply a structuration of affect and of the social order in which he is at a loss, because he is at a loss for words. The warrior takes what he wants, or as Cavell puts it, Coriolanus avoids "asking for something . . . by . . . deserving the thing," which he establishes through his valor, through physical force (154). In contrast, at the court, in the courtroom, or in the marketplace, a person must negotiate to get what she wants. And to negotiate, she must associate, or mingle, with others; if she is to be successful, she must carefully attune herself to the words and gestures of others, weighing her own words as well as theirs, whether or not they are her social equals.[12] She cannot allow her heart to be her mouth, as Coriolanus does: "What his breast forges, that his tongue must vent; / And being angry, does forget that ever / He heard the name of death" (III.i.256–58).

It is, therefore, especially appropriate that Coriolanus's outbursts against "mingling them with us" occur as he is on his way to the marketplace. Significantly, I think, Shakespeare associates Coriolanus's fears—of words, of negotiation, of exchange—with the political demands of his social inferiors and not with the requirements of a court that is becoming increasingly civilized, restrained, and subdued. This move obscures the extent to which the conflict in *Coriolanus* is both inter- and intrastatus conflict, thus encouraging structurally the kind of political criticism that has characterized the play: left versus right, radical versus conservative.

Perhaps better than some critics, Coriolanus understands those evolving requirements of the court; the play's numerous allusions to acting and policy and the need for gentle words and self-control suggest as much, and Menenius and Volumnia in particular spend considerable effort in trying to convince the retrograde warrior of the desirability of heeding them. And ironically, even as Coriolanus insists upon the dangers of blurring the absolute distinction between plebeians and patricians ("You are plebeians / If they be senators"), the hot warrior points to new ways, more subtle ways of separating and distinguishing superiors and subordinates, ways that will be well suited to a society in which hegemony will be established through intellectual rather than physical power.

That is, when Coriolanus asserts that "dishonour / Mangles true judgement, and bereaves the state / Of that integrity which should become't"

(III.i.156–58), he suggests, as argued above, that true judgment depends on the maintaining of distinction. When distinction dissolves, so does judgment. But *mangle* is related in one of its senses to style, and particularly to verbal style. Failing to maintain distinction, allowing the multitude voice, results in mistakes, misrecognition, blundering, and falsification, whether of pronunciation or in the transmission of written texts, as the *OED* suggests. Mingling with the crowd renders a "true" judgment unrecognizable; poorly executed, such a judgment can only be in bad taste—or laughable, a judgment not to be treated seriously.

Here indeed, as Patterson suggests, the question seems to be one of power—the word itself appears more often in *Coriolanus* than in any other play ("thirty-eight appearances, as compared to eighteen in *Richard II*, the closest competitor"); and yet, despite the prowess of the lead character, power in *Coriolanus* refers most often to political power, not physical force (*Voice* 141). Thus, when Adelman asserts that we identify with Coriolanus because of power, his claim to independence, she cannot mean that "we" identify with the manner or basis of his power, enforced by his "sword, death's stamp" (II.ii.107), but with his power per se. Adelman "delight[s] in his claim" because as an intellectual and as member of the upper middle class, she, too, holds considerable social power, social power based not in a sword but in a pen. (Nor is it difficult to imagine the literary intellectual's version of self-sufficiency and omnipotence: an audience who buys every word you write.)

In *Coriolanus*, as Patterson argues, Shakespeare does address the question of social power, and in constructing his warrior's failure, his tragedy, Shakespeare points to style as the proper form of domination; Coriolanus's tragedy is that he cannot or will not master a political style appropriate to the modern world. Social power, *Coriolanus* tells us, will henceforth be distributed differently: self-evident, absolute distinction based on blood will give way to constructed distinction based on style, which takes great time and effort to establish and maintain and thus is not available to most people, as Weber, Veblen, Elias, Levine, Guillory, Woodmansee, and Bourdieu all remind us. Of manners, for example, Bourdieu explains that they

> owe their value to the fact that they manifest the rarest conditions of acquisition, that is, a social power over time which is tacitly recognized as the supreme excellence: to possess things from the past, i.e., accumulated, crystallized history, aristocratic names and titles, chateaux or "stately homes," paintings and collections, vintage wines and antique furniture, is to master time, through all those things whose common feature is that they can only

be acquired in the course of time, by means of time, against time, that is, by inheritance or through dispositions which, like the taste for old things, are likewise only acquired with time and applied by those who can take their time. (*Distinction* 71–72)

Under circumstances like these, to enlarge the franchise, redefine the meaning of representation, or provide the people a handful of tribunes "to defend their vulgar wisdoms" (I.i.214) is hardly to threaten established hierarchies of power or patterns of inequality. According to Bristol, "the opposition between Coriolanus and the tribunate is . . . mediated by the framing social reality of the *res publica* as a lawfully constituted form of social life. . . . [a] constitutional settlement [that] brings with it a more or less stable legitimation of an ensemble of power relations" ("Lenten" 211).[13] Indeed, the play makes clear that Coriolanus stands alone in resisting what has been newly granted to the plebeians, even as it makes clear that Coriolanus is no authority on political speech. Other patricians seem not to be overly disturbed by working with the tribunes, and Menenius engages with them—as he engages with the plebeians themselves—in banter that is charged but restrained, a style that acknowledges the tribunes' support within the political elite whose respect Menenius values, or at least feels he should value ("I must be content to bear with those that say you are reverend grave men" [II.i.59–60].)

Coriolanus resolves the problem of giving people voice by ensuring that what is spoken will be tightly circumscribed through representation, in short, that someone else will speak for the people—a perhaps timely reminder for Shakespeare's contemporaries of what is central as political elections slowly replace political selections.[14] Patterson admits as much in rejecting the conservative claim that "by making the tribunes unacceptable Shakespeare was warning his nation against classical republicanism" (*Voice* 132). This rejection she defends by reminding us that even "modern democracies are riddled with such types, that electoral politics depend on the manipulation of the electorate, and that the tribunes represent, in particular, a noxious form of the left-wing intellectual's dilemma—that leadership, coming from above, is difficult to distinguish from exploitation" (*Voice* 132). With this last, I certainly agree, and it is significant that Patterson bases her defense here of a liberal Shakespeare on the assumed value of our own liberal, representative democracies. Yet as Bristol reminds us, "a constitution does not resolve the conflicts built into the division of social labor" ("Lenten" 211) and from another point of view, such as that of the majority of people who "survive" the politics that is "done" to them, the value of representative democracy is not obvious.

Patterson wants to tell a story about Shakespeare "with maximum force and economy," a story that seeks to situate Shakespeare within a recoverable history in order to contest the largely conservative stories told of him since the early nineteenth century (*Voice* 10, 122, 153). Confident of her story, its force and economy and historical accuracy, Patterson can demand that the conservative but hegemonic "version of *Coriolanus* . . . be put in its place," presumably, the trash bin or the history book (*Voice* 153). But despite the judgments of some literary theory, all is not discourse, and even if, as in Terence Hawkes's formulation, "we mean by Shakespeare" (*Meaning* 3), by the stories we tell about Shakespeare, the crucial question remains: whose story? Who means by Shakespeare? Hawkes? Patterson? Coleridge? Hazlitt? me? One or another of that represented majority might say to Patterson or to Hawkes or to me what the first citizen says to Menenius, who also wants to tell "a pretty tale": "Well, I'll hear it, sir; yet you must not think to fob off our disgrace with a tale" (I.i.92–93). For the merely represented, for the disgraced, a story about Shakespeare will not do.

Even a sympathetic story will not do.[15] The analysis of ventriloquism—what Patterson defines as "evidence . . . of the popular voice raised in articulate protest [that] has come down to us . . . in the texts of the dominant culture"— may be the best we can do to infer otherwise unwritten voices of the past, and Patterson is correct to argue that some texts of the dominant culture do a better job than others of speaking for the people (*Voice* 41, 46). But even the best ventriloquist requires a dummy, a thing that does not speak, a thing that is manipulated. Even the best ventriloquist does not know whereof he speaks, cannot know what the dummy feels, which is why Hammond, a coal miner, became a delegate to the 1992 Democratic National Convention: "the people who are best qualified to speak about the issues of working people are the working people themselves" (152). Hammond wanted a voice; he wanted to influence what would become the Clinton administration on behalf of himself and others in the working class. But he found that after the song and dance of the campaign was over, no one in the Democratic Party or at the Democratic National Committee was interested in listening to him, especially not the "Ivy League suit-boys" who "are now running the country" (153).

This chapter begins with stories, a story about my mom and the stories she told, and the chapter ends with stories, stories about Shakespeare and stories about *Coriolanus,* stories about voice, about who has voice and who does not. My story about *Coriolanus* has been this: the play refigures distinction, previously established as something absolute, as something negotiable—as style, as politics—and fobs off on the people the notion that political representation will make them players in such negotiations. Coriolanus's failure, his tragedy, is that he is not prepared to negotiate with the plebeians, or even with their representatives.[16]

It is here, I think, that "we" are like Coriolanus. Like Coriolanus, we are not prepared to negotiate with people who are not like us—not socially powerful, not serious, not mannered, not tasteful, not discriminating. We rely on institutions to mediate those negotiations for us—systems of education, protocols of professionalism, the various mechanisms of representative democracy, even trade unions—mediating institutions that inescapably rig the negotiations in our favor by humiliating those who remain formally outside them. When we do not tell their stories ourselves, we, like Coriolanus, receive their voices and their stories as "shreds" (I.i.207). Mingling mangles.

I wish to conclude with another story. At the 1995 MLA convention in Chicago, the MLA delegate assembly passed an emergency resolution proposing to "censure Yale University administration for permitting the use of union activity as a criterion for academic evaluations and for failing to protect the right of Yale's graduate teaching staff to participate in union activities, including job actions, without fear of reprisals against their academic careers" (MLA mailing, 9 February 1996, 3). Subsequently, much has been written about this matter, and distributed over the Internet and in print, including more than half of an issue of *Social Text*, an expanded version of which became *Will Teach for Food: Academic Labor in Crisis*, edited by tenured radical Cary Nelson. Before the MLA membership voted on the resolution, members were invited to contribute arguments in favor or against the resolution, and many did. One eloquent defender of Yale is the Karl Young Professor of English at Yale, Annabel Patterson, who writes to set the record straight about what caused this rift between Yale and its graduate students and how the university and its faculty have responded to the students' attempts at unionization, one of which involved becoming a "wing of Locals 34 and 35 of the Hotel Employees and Restaurant Employees International Union." Concerning this affiliation, Patterson points out the difficulty it brings, because "Yale is not prepared to negotiate academic policy, such as the structure of the teaching program or class size, with the Hotel Employees and Restaurant Employees International Union," who "draw their membership from the dining workers in the colleges and other support staff" ("Letter" 6).

Yale is not prepared to negotiate academic policy with representatives of hotel and restaurant workers. Doubtless Yale ain't, and Patterson musters much rhetorical power to emphasize that point, although not to justify it.

Indeed, Patterson's use of "prepared" is wonderfully ironic, since the word's principal meaning suggests, even in Patterson's syntax although not in her context, that Yale just hasn't done its homework, that an extension of time might allow Yale to get prepared. But Patterson means, of course, that Yale is not *inclined* under any circumstances to negotiate with the union. ("As if/in your dreams" the sentence seems to say, underscoring the impossibility of such negotiation by the use of a word that on the surface invokes its possibility.) To be so prepared, so inclined to negotiate, dare I suggest, is as unthinkable, as preposterous to Patterson as mingling with the plebeians is to Coriolanus.

My aim here is not to attack or insult Patterson who, it seems to me, deserves the status in the academy she has achieved. Nor do I wish (necessarily or entirely) to disagree with her; I, too, want my support staff to be supportive and my hotel workers to make up my bed, not my syllabus. Even less do I wish to give too much sympathy or uncritical support to the graduate students at Yale. If I align Patterson with Coriolanus, I do not align the graduate students with the plebeians, not when, in 1996, in addition to tuition and health insurance, they received $9,940 per year for two years to do course work, a sum they would receive in their third and fourth years for teaching half-time (Eakin 56). These numbers are the lowest I have seen reported, but even so, when extrapolated to a full-time, yearlong job, remuneration at such rates would approach $35,000, exclusive of benefits—"hardly a sweatshop wage," as one journalist points out (Palmaffy 20). Margaret Homans, another defender of Yale—and another object of mockery by Michael Bérubé (42–48)—is nevertheless correct in this: "it is not possible for Yale students—in training, after all, to occupy professional positions—to constitute the proletarianized body they claim to be" (11).[17]

Nor is my aim here to assess either the academic labor market, which I have attempted elsewhere ("Stars"), or the profession's relationships to (organized) labor. Regarding the latter, however, I do agree with Richard Rorty that to deal seriously with labor and the problems of workers, the profession "would have to transform itself" (91). For professors, this would mean, for instance, training oneself not to turn questions of class into questions of culture and, furthermore, as I argue throughout this book, not to see only red when the question of class arises. It would mean facing up to the ways educational institutions—and in particular elite institutions like Yale—maintain and reinforce structured inequality through their control of occupational opportunities and through their control of cultural authority.

I invoke Patterson's defense of Yale because it reveals what is one of the purposes of this book to point out: a gap between an academic elite's left-leaning political desires, which seep deeply into its work, its criticism, and that same elite's actual exercise of power and dominance in the world. According to Ohmann, our profession is "organized . . . to regulate careers and maintain hierarchies of status among practitioners and institutions" (*English* xlvi). And therefore, as Guillory observes, universities "are by no means structurally organized to express the consensus of a community; these social and institutional sites are complex hierarchies in which the position and privilege of judgment are objects of competitive struggles" (*Capital* 27). Under such conditions the dining room worker at Yale has no voice, and neither does the adjunct professor at Troy State University or even the tenured professor at Clarion University, as Terry Caesar explained over a decade ago. None of these can judge because none has competed successfully. The professor who has competed successfully cannot change those facts or those conditions by telling a story. She must be prepared to negotiate, to act. To this possibility I turn in the next chapter. As we shall see in discussing the politics of pastoral and enclosure, of environmentalism and cultural tourism, upper-middle-class intellectuals remain unconcerned about the lives and opportunities of working-class people. Negotiation with people like these is an act for which the upper middle class simply is not prepared.

CHAPTER FIVE

Shakespeare in the Woods

The Class Politics of Cultural Tourism

*I*n "Patronage and the Economics of the Theater," which appears in John D. Cox and David Scott Kastan's *A New History of Early English Drama*, Kathleen E. McLuskie and Felicity Dunsworth remind us that there is "a gap between the smooth, artistically satisfying conceptualization of social change and the much slower and more muddled and contradictory pace of change in institutional structures and social relations." Far from disabling the search for meaning, however, such a gap is where "meanings can be made." Concerning the economics of the early modern theater, "what the meanings are will depend on how the writer theorizes the relations between money and artistic freedom, between economic and ideological relations, between the histories of the past and the present" (439).

An empiricist might object that McLuskie and Dunsworth leave too much to theory, and a theorist might object that they fail to theorize the relation between neat conceptualizations and messy facts, but for my purposes here it is enough to recognize the accuracy of their statement: for most of us most of the time, the meanings we generate do depend on how we theorize certain (empirical) relationships. That we do this accounts for the persistence of interpretation in the face of contradictory facts, and it allows for the kind of analysis I attempt in this chapter, which contests the generation of meaning by questioning the theorizing going on in the gap, although my focus is not patronage but an intersection of four related discourses: on the one hand, enclosure and pastoral, and on the other hand, environmentalism and cultural tourism.

Edward Bond, the contemporary playwright, is not alone in worrying about Shakespeare and what Patterson calls "those ambiguous records relating to enclosures" (*Voice* 2). Critics worry about what Shakespeare was doing in the woods outside Stratford because we have determined that participation in "enclosure is *invariably* a negative" (W. Carroll 36), a blot on a person's moral, if not financial, life. So settled is this opinion that whether one defends Shakespeare or condemns him, Shakespeare's goodness depends on how one assesses his—or his plays'—attitude toward enclosure, the displacement of rural populations, and the concentration of power over land use into the hands of an elite few.

For example, Wilson thinks Shakespeare records the sentiments of the powerful and the victorious, sentiments that, it is essential to note, can and often do include acknowledgment of the distress of the losers, in this case the displaced. History therefore records repeated attempts by the Crown and Parliament to regulate enclosure in order to defuse public demonstrations or rioting. And in plays like *As You Like It,* Shakespeare is "unequivocal" about the negative effects of enclosure—"depopulation, arson and, as Adam says, 'butchery' of those who dare resist" (*Power* 68)—but at the same time, he is unequivocal about the benefits of enclosure, in particular to the rising middling sort to which he belonged and who were, as John Walter suggests, unlikely to support the protests of the displaced, those "whose declared aim was to challenge the agrarian capitalism which underwrote their growing wealth and power" (122). In contrast, Patterson defends Shakespeare from such charges, arguing that the evidence does not "justify our drawing the conclusion that a man who moves upwards on the social scale is inevitably proud of that move, to the point of invariably defending the class divisions in his society and denigrating what he has left behind" (*Voice* 2).

In what is perhaps the most recent attempt to problematize enclosure, William C. Carroll identifies the theorizing that settles opinion on this issue as a "nostalgic vision—one might almost say fantasy—of an always already lost communal perfection" (35). Carroll argues cogently against the judgment that enclosures were invariably initiated by the wealthy and powerful, men motivated by greed and determined to dispossess their otherwise happy and cooperative tenants (35). Of course, such a point was made in the 1950s by Joan Thirsk and, in different fashion, by Alan Macfarlane in the 1970s. But one can go further: the open-field system of farming itself hardly approximated "communal perfection." As Tawney pointed out in 1912, for these farmers, "the word common implies common exclusiveness quite as much as common enjoyment" ("Agrarian" 238). Or, as economist Carl J. Dahlman explained in 1980, the commons were both communal and private property ("they were private for a group, but communal for members of that group") and such an organization of the commons, based in mixed property rights, strikingly resembles that of a modern corporation (203, 204–5), which is not the kind of enterprise normally seen to stimulate thoughts of "communal perfection" in the minds of literary or cultural critics.

That Carroll identifies a latent or quasi Marxism as nostalgic or fantastical is interesting, even perhaps, amusing. But as an explanation for received critical opinion on enclosure, for what fills the gap, I find it less than satisfactory, because, as Susan Bennett points out, collective nostalgia of this sort is invariably conservative and hobbles analysis of what becomes in comparison "a defective and diminished present" (5). Whether coming from the political Left or Right, such nostalgia "insists on the preservation of a specified version of a constructed past" (161 n. 4). In this case, what is preserved are two notions: on the one hand, that the open-field system of farming represented or realized "communal perfection" and, on the other, that enclosure was an inevitable and necessary, if painful, ingredient in the transition to capitalism (and therefore, or so goes the teleology, in the transition to socialism). From this perspective, the social effects of enclosure are not unlike those of contemporary deindustrialization and the globalization of the industrial economy: painful indeed for the victims, but inevitable.

In this defective and diminished present, however, attempts are made nevertheless to achieve these nostalgic visions of "communal perfection." People in the state of Oregon are famous for one such attempt, a series of efforts—some legal, some attitudinal—that might be summed up in the bumper sticker that says: "Don't Californicate Oregon." Comparison of Oregon with the behemoth to the south is revelatory: gone is the unrestricted development, the intrusions of inexpensive housing developments, supersized Wal-Marts, gas stations, used-car lots, billboards. Not much there disturbs the natural environment, and the contrast with California is shocking, shocking even with that very mellow, almost Oregonian subset of California, the Humboldt Nation.[1]

Also just north of the border sits the Oregon Shakespeare Festival, located in Ashland—a small, picturesque town that is not far from the wild and scenic Rogue River and over which towers seventy-five-hundred-foot Mt. Ashland. Thirty or even twenty years ago, Ashland's economy and built environment, like those of other towns in Jackson and Josephine counties, was dominated by those who lived off the extraction of natural resources from the surrounding heavily forested mountain areas: the families of millworkers and owners, of truck drivers and loggers. Today, Ashland is dominated by those who live off of William Shakespeare. During its eight-month season, the OSF draws over 350,000 people into its three theaters and generates over 90 million dollars for the local economy. In town are numerous businesses that can "see how this world / goes with no eyes" and have inferred, correctly, that when "the great one . . . goes upward, let him draw thee after" (*King Lear* IV.vi.148–49, II.iv.71–72): All's Well Herb and Vitamin Shop; Arden Forest Inn; Bard's Inn

Motel Best Western; Bloomsbury Books; Mark Antony Hotel; Miller Renaissance Landscaping and Design; Mind's Eye Juice Bar; Paddington Station Emporium; Puck's Doughnuts; Renaissance Chiropractic Clinic; Romeo Inn, Shakespeare Book Store; and Shrew's House, among many others.

This transformation—from (working-class) logging center to (upper-middle-class) cultural tourism[2] center—did not occur overnight. Nor is such transformation limited to southern Oregon; it is characteristic of life today in most of the Pacific Northwest and indeed of the West generally—in New Mexico, Colorado, and Utah as well as in Idaho, Washington, and Oregon. And I do not wish to suggest that the OSF—its patrons, its administrative staff, or its artistic or production companies—actively engaged in abetting this transformation, as in, say, determining "let's kill all the loggers" (cf. *2 Henry VI*). But it is clear that from the beginning, the two industries would have little in common, as this anecdote from an OSF website reveals:

> The story goes that when [festival founder Angus] Bowmer asked around the town for assistance and materials to build a stage, he approached the owner of a local mill. The miller scoffed at him and threw down a single piece of wood, telling him he could have that. ("Oregon Shakespeare Festival")

More than sixty years later, in the nicely landscaped courtyard of the OSF in Ashland, that single piece of wood is displayed prominently, reminding us that we are about to enter "America's First Elizabethan Theatre." It is a symbol not just of one man's determination but of a cultural and economic struggle between producers of (basic) commodities and producers of culture and leisure. It is a struggle that has been repeated with different players—ecotourists or kayakers or software programmers instead of Shakespeareans—throughout the West.

That the producers of culture and leisure have won this struggle is also clear: falling living standards among the working class are one strong indicator of this and, in Ashland, so is Shakespeare's omnipresence. Shakespeare nourishes the forests around Ashland and the forests, in turn, nourish the OSF's patrons, becoming the West Coast's upper-middle-class green world, as former artistic director Henry Woronicz celebrates:

> The energy released each season by this process of communion, by our artists and audience, has seeped into the soil of Ashland. It has become part of the landscape, the trees and hills. It has become the source and power of

the yearly pilgrimages to these special theaters. It draws us back, each year, to the magic of Ashland, the glory of Shakespeare, witnessing the bold energy and the unyielding spirit of the theatrical imagination. (2)

Woronicz's understanding of the OSF's relationship to its audience emphasizes two sources of appeal. First is the equating of Shakespeare with God, or at the very least, the equating of Ashland and the OSF with a sacred religious site, a judgment seconded by current artistic director Libby Appel, who enthuses that "theatre is really a religious experience" (2). Actors and audiences are pilgrims, making yearly visits to Ashland to commune with the glory that is Shakespeare. Of course, the sacralization of Shakespeare is not new. For quite some time—a century or two—Shakespeare has been "the name of a tutelary deity or cult-object," and since the eighteenth century, pilgrims have desired—and entrepreneurs have provided—relics of the Bard, what we now call souvenirs: fragments from the famous mulberry tree have metamorphosed into items such as an "Out, damned spot!" eraser or a "To do or not to Do" notepad (Bristol, *America* 19; Hodgdon 209, 232).

It is important to acknowledge, as do Bristol and Levine, that the sacralization of Shakespeare is not wholly phony or merely a mechanism of social control. But neither is it an accurate description of Shakespeare's essence. As in the nineteenth century, so now: perceived social and cultural flux causes people to yearn for stability, and because of the legal separation of church and state, as well as a decline in religiosity generally, Americans identify educational and cultural institutions as sites where it is possible to order a "universe of strangers" (Levine 177). Bristol considers "fantastical" the idea that a "curriculum based on a substantive *literary* culture can become a functional equivalent for religion" (*America* 60), but fear can spawn fantastical ideas, and both Bristol and Levine recognize as key to this fear the threat of the masses, hundreds of millions of people who prefer, for instance, that their entertainment strut horsepower rather than "a poor player, / . . . upon the stage" (*Macbeth* V.v.24–25).

A second source of appeal for audiences is Ashland's provision of something we cannot get at home, whether that home be in Portland, Seattle, San Francisco, or most certainly, Los Angeles. Implying a contrast with the cement and steel, the pollution and congestion of our urban or suburban neighborhoods and workplaces, Woronicz invites us to dwell upon the appeal of the soil, of the trees and hills, all of which absorb the energy of "artists and audience" and which, like a savings bank or maybe a health spa, return that energy to those who return year after year.

Yet to dwell on this appeal leads a Shakespearean to dwell on the ancient and contemporary meanings of pastoral, a literary discourse that addresses the relationship of humans to nature. As a literary phenomenon, pastoral is notoriously difficult to pin down, which is perhaps not surprising given its long history: in writing the *Eclogues,* claims Patterson, Virgil "established the principle that genuine imitation, especially of pastoral, always remakes its object in a new historical context" (*Pastoral* 39). Still, such remakings have proliferated remarkably, especially since the late eighteenth century and in the wake of what appears to be an unstoppable urbanization or rather, to use a current political buzzword, urban sprawl: if in early modern England 90 percent of the population resided in rural settings and "sheep outnumbered people, perhaps by as many as three to one" (Montrose, "Pastoral" 421), today in the United States perhaps only 2 or 3 percent of the people farm and almost no one herds sheep. In such a society, in which "wilderness" is at once a powerful icon and a chimera,[3] "pastoral" has become pervasive, restricted no longer to the "obsolescent conventions of the eclogue tradition, but . . . [available to] all literature—poetry or prose, fiction or nonfiction—that celebrates the ethos of nature/rurality over against the ethos of the town or city. This domain includes . . . all degrees of rusticity from farm to wilderness" (Buell, "Pastoral" 23 n. 1).

Arguably, however, the kind of work that prompts Lawrence Buell's expansive definition of pastoral has not led to better understanding of the form or of the concerns central to it: indeed, the "irritant" that moves Paul Alpers to his recent book-length reassessment of pastoral is precisely this "ungoverned inclusiveness" in our use of the term (ix), what Patterson, alluding to William Empson's famous work, calls our tendency to "search for 'versions of pastoral' in the most unlikely places" (*Pastoral* 7). I sympathize with and even support Alpers's disciplinary impulse—"a literary definition is revealing and useful, it seems to me, not when it plants its banner everywhere but when it is clear about what does and does not count as an example of the phenomenon in question" (ix)—but I also recognize, as I am sure Alpers does, that the meanings of pastoral, like those of other literary discourses such as tragedy or romance, are not monopolized and cannot be policed effectively by the discipline. Pastoral is as much a cultural as a literary discourse—indeed, perhaps nowadays more cultural than literary—but in any case, its power as a cultural discourse helps to generate the proliferation of meanings within literary discourse to which Alpers objects.

In this sense, Alpers's analysis echoes somewhat that of Leo Marx in his work on pastoral in America, which distinguishes "between two kinds of pastoralism—one that is popular and sentimental, the other imaginative and complex" (5). This distinction Marx further refined as that between what he calls a "primitive ideal" and a "pastoral ideal":

> both seem to originate in a recoil from the pain and responsibility of life in a complex civilization—the familiar impulse to withdraw from the city, locus of power and politics, into nature. The difference is that the primitivist hero keeps going, as it were, so that eventually he locates value as far as possible, in space or time or both, from organized society; the shepherd, on the other hand, seeks a resolution of the conflict between the opposed worlds of nature and art. (22)

Alpers is familiar, of course, with the lessons of postmodernism and presumably therefore less subject to the class and cultural biases of a previous generation. Unlike Marx, Alpers is careful not to identify "the people" as the source of a "simple" pastoralism that, through the embrace of a binary opposing country to city, has undermined the power of an "imaginative and complex" literary pastoralism. Rather, Alpers argues, the construction of such a binary within literature, which focuses attention inappropriately on the landscape, and in particular, on an idealized nature associated with "the Golden Age, innocence, and nostalgia" (28), originates in Schiller's *On Naive and Sentimental Poetry,* a work whose theory is appropriated, embodied in poetry, and ultimately institutionalized by the English Romantic poets and their Victorian successors.[4]

It is beyond the scope of this chapter to summarize the theoretical and historical arguments of Alpers, Marx, Patterson, or for that matter, Empson or Louis Montrose, but the key problem for all, I think, is the binarism that, in Buell's formulation, sets "nature/rurality over against . . . the town or city" and, as a corollary, flattens "nature" into a category that, depending on the needs of the writer, can be identified exclusively with a wilderness untouched by human beings or, alternatively, can accommodate a family farm in Ohio, corporate agriculture in California's central valley, and a Shakespeare festival in Central Park or among the redwoods at a university in Santa Cruz, California. This diversity in pastoral writers' definitions of "nature/rurality" resembles that in contemporary ecological critique, which constitutes a continuum of tolerance for production or extraction, for the human touch, in wild and rural areas. It is a continuum that ranges from the nearly zero tolerance of environmental resistance groups such as Earth First! to the rather full tolerance of the various "wise use" groups, which, despite serious differences (for example, whether "wise use" is to be achieved by preserving federal subsidies or by preserving property rights and access to a free market), generally "hold fast to the view that the only worthy economic pursuits are those that 'produce real wealth,' meaning wealth extracted from the land" through logging, mining, and farming (Snow 29).

So, while one can easily imagine a Wise User's invoking of classical and biblical justification for what historian Keith Thomas calls "human ascendancy" and "the subjugation of the natural world" (17, 25), one can just as easily imagine Earth First! cofounder Dave Foreman's approving of judgments by contemporary ecoliterary critics, such as Joseph Meeker's that "what the pastoral tradition calls 'nature' is merely simplified civilization" (90) or Glenn A. Love's that "a viable pastoral for the future might well find its healing vision not in the simplicity of the garden, but in the complexity of the old-growth forest" (205). Just as easily, too, one can imagine politically mainstream, upper-middle-class friends of the Nature Conservancy on a Saturday morning walk near Palm Springs, California, winding their way to an oasis formed by the San Andreas fault zone. One can imagine that, once there and settled among the thickly trunked palms, which surround pools of water forced upwards between tectonic plates, these women and men might find much to approve in the effects of Shakespeare's pastoral plays, which, as Rosalie Colie explains, focus on aristocratic characters' exile from a civilized but corrupt court, their "recreative sojourn in a natural setting," and their "ultimate return 'homeward' from the exile, a return in moral strength reinforced by the country experiences of kind and kindness" (245). The oasis offers just such possibilities for recreative sojourn: along with hot springs, golf courses, tennis courts, and the ministrations of resort and restaurant staffs, the oasis is a necessary part of an early-twenty-first-century weekend retreat, "a place of *otium*—leisure—through which one might refresh oneself for the next, inevitable round of *negotium*" (Schama 530).

Regardless of this definitional diversity, what unites the various strands of contemporary ecological critique (including even that of the Wise Users) is what unites post-Romantic pastoral: "rigid divisions of nature and society or humanity and ecology" (Luke xix). To be sure, the idealization of nature implicit in such binaries is itself (potentially) a mode of social criticism, but as Dave Foreman or the theorists of deep ecology know, it is criticism of "a special sort, based . . . on retrenchment, renunciation, and retreat" (Young 28). And it is this sort of idealism, idealism as withdrawal, as requiring a return "to the Pleistocene era for some premodern perfection" (Luke 202), that leads certain thinkers—not just literary critics but ecologists, historians, and political activists—to unsettle the binary and to acknowledge what Harry Berger Jr. calls the "dangerous or sinister side" of pastoral's natural or "green" world (15).

What is sinister about the green world is not just that, as Colie remarks, "violence [is] required to make persuasive . . . the tale of restoration—so that one finds a high degree of cruelty and brutality (often very schematically and unemotionally wielded) around the edges of pastoral romance, in both narrative and dramatic forms" (284–85). No, it is not just the hardness of nature, nor the wolves, snakes, and lions that frequent these imaginative tales, nor even the outbreaks in them of violence or near violence on the part of humans, that makes the green world sinister, as Berger famously argues, and as I quote at some length:

> The green world seems to possess two essential qualities: first, since it is only metaphorically a place or space, it embodies a condition whose value should not remain fixed but should rather change according to the temporal process of which it is a part. It appears first as exemplary or appealing and lures us away from the evil or confusion of everyday life. But when it has fulfilled its moral, esthetic, social, cognitive, or experimental functions, it becomes inadequate and its creator turns us out. Those who wish to remain, who cannot or will not be discharged, are presented as in some way deficient. Thus the second quality of the green world is that it is ambiguous: its usefulness and dangers arise from the same source. In its positive aspects it provides a temporary haven for recreation or clarification, experiment or relief; in its negative aspects it projects the urge of the paralyzed will to give up, escape, work magic, abolish time and flux and the intrusive reality of other minds. (36)

To "abolish time and flux": in pastoral governed by Marx's "primitive ideal" or a binary that privileges an idealized nature, something is missing—the shepherd, the human figure, and thus time and history. Complex forms of pastoral recognize and accept that "history cannot be stopped" (L. Marx 72). Similarly, moderate environmentalists recognize that the privileging of wild, untouched nature within a binary is itself "a product of the very history it seeks to deny" (Cronon 39). Such a wilderness—"entirely a creation of the culture that holds it dear"—embodies "the illusion that we can somehow wipe clean the slate of our past and return to the tabula rasa that supposedly existed before we began to leave our marks on the world." Like its historical antecedent, the green world, wilderness potentially embodies a desire to deny history or to escape from it (Cronon 39, 40).

Alpers's project is to recuperate a "pre-Romantic poetics of pastoral, to which not nature but certain kinds of human beings and human experience are central" (37). His is not, however, a solitary battle, and Alpers marshals for support a strong if not dominant tradition of modern work on pastoral that emphasizes time, history, and politics. Including work by Empson, Burke, Williams, Patterson, and Montrose, this tradition reminds us, as both Alpers and Montrose say of Empson, that pastoral as literary form expresses not only individual psychology but also and more importantly social relationships, in particular of inequality, inequality filtered through representations of the land and of power over its use.

Since the beginning, issues of land use—the threat of its loss or of eviction from it—have been central to pastoral, either directly, in terms of content, or indirectly, in terms of ideological force. Critics sometimes refer to Virgil's first eclogue as "The Dispossessed," and we know the poem reprises a traumatic episode in the poet's life, in which his own lands were seized to reward the soldiers of the victorious emperor, Octavian (L. Marx 20; Schama 528; Patterson, *Pastoral* 134). Such threats, however, are not always imagined, nor are they visited only on poets vulnerable to the whims of patrons and princes. Precisely because "poets have often lent their tongues to princes," the poet can be the agent or the beneficiary of loss and eviction: "it is not easy to forget that Sidney's *Arcadia,* which gives a continuing title to English neo-pastoral, was written in a park which had been made by enclosing a whole village and evicting the tenants" (Williams, *City* 22). Williams underscores the point with which I began this chapter: even in the sixteenth century, enclosure and dispossession was not always achieved in the interests of rationalized agrarian capitalism. Nor was it subsequently; in the eighteenth century, during a "massive reorganization of landownership," which dispossessed thousands, enclosure "was frequently performed in the service of the gentleman's park" (Patterson, *Pastoral* 195).

Yet Williams also is wrong: we do forget these facts, the interconnection of art and inequality, and we forget them rather easily. Pastoral itself, as Empson suggests, aids our forgetfulness: the form's "essential trick" is to "imply a beautiful relation between rich and poor" by making "simple people express strong feelings . . . in learned and fashionable language" (11). The trick allows the author or reader to think "better of both" and more importantly, to incorporate into the self "the merits of the two sorts" of people (12). Yet because, as Empson acknowledges, pastoral is "about" the people but not produced or consumed by them (6), because, that is, "the representative strengths of aristocratic and peasant values and styles are combined—but only for the benefit of the peasant's betters" (Montrose, "Pastoral" 417), the tendency of pastoral's representations of social relationships is to mediate or occlude or, as Burke puts it, stylistically transcend the inequalities at hand (*Motives* 124). Indeed,

Burke judged that "one will look long among the writings of most self-professed 'Marxist' critics before he finds such profoundly Marxist analysis of literature" as Empson's (*Form* 424).

Burke's enthusiasm notwithstanding, Empson has been much criticized for emphasizing this social function of pastoral, so much so that even today, after twenty years of feminism, deconstruction, new historicism, and multiculturalism, the line cited most often to encapsulate *Some Versions of Pastoral* is one that reduces the argument to formal considerations: pastoral is a "process of putting the complex into the simple" (22). Tempting as it might be to attribute such a distillation entirely to the ideological needs of an earlier ahistoricist critical practice, it is best to resist the urge, for at least some of the critical resistance to the social analysis of *Versions* must be located in the book's analytic oversimplifications. Our debt to Empson (and Burke) notwithstanding, I think Montrose and Patterson are correct to urge more sophisticated understandings of the relationships between social formations and literary forms. With respect to early modern England in particular, Empson's "conception of a rigid dichotomy of economic class—the rich and the poor—misrepresents the multiple and overlapping status hierarchies of Elizabethan society, and the connotations of a pastoral 'trick' are too crudely conspiratorial to describe the complex mediations through which cultural forms and social relations are reciprocally shaped" (Montrose, "Pastoral" 417; Patterson, *Pastoral* 133–40).

The problem is that to identify the social location of Elizabethan pastoral is not to identify the ideological workings of the form; it is to identify where one begins to look for and assess ideological work. To be sure, to speak of pastoral is to speak of high culture, of the property of a tiny ruling elite, but early modern English pastoral is "ideological" not just because of this fact—because it transforms into courtly games and baubles the hardness of rural and agrarian life, and therefore reveals, according to Williams, "more connection . . . with the real interests of the court than with country life in any of its possible forms" (*City* 21). Rather (and this, it seems to me, is the crux of Montrose's and Patterson's attempts to complicate Empson and Williams), early modern English pastoral is "ideological" because it serves different purposes for different people. Thus, according to Montrose, "literary pastoralization involves not only a process by which agrarian social relations are inscribed within an ideology of the country but also a process by which that initial inscription is itself appropriated, transformed, and reinscribed within an ideology of the court" ("Pastoral" 431). Within both of these processes, pastoral serves a variety of functions and interests, including those of the monarch, the nobility, aspirants to such status, politicians, and writers and intellectuals. Although certainly ideological, "Elizabethan pastoral discourse is . . . not reducible to a particular ideology" (Montrose, "Pastoral" 420).

And yet: in responding to arguments such as these that complicate "simplistic and unhistorical" or "strictly partisan" formulations of the workings of pastoral and of power (Montrose, "Pastoral" 419; Patterson, *Pastoral* 139), I find myself positioned vis-à-vis Montrose and Patterson as, perhaps, they found themselves positioned vis-à-vis Empson and Williams. That is to say, Montrose and Patterson profess sympathy with the political impulses and aims of projects that, in the name of rigor, each seeks to amend. Patterson is motivated not "to challenge in its broad outlines the premise that seventeenth-century pastoral was ideologically the property of the most privileged class" (*Pastoral* 139), just as Montrose is motivated not "to apologize" for the aristocratic appropriation of Elizabethan pastoral discourse ("Pastoral" 420). Still, each thinks the workings of the pastoral discourse at issue are more complicated than the "broad outlines" might suggest.

Similarly, as I have already indicated above, I sympathize with projects such as Montrose's or Patterson's that aim to complicate our understandings of the workings of power; this book is intended to further such efforts. And yet—the same yet with which I began the previous paragraph—I worry about the ideological effects of work that dulls this particular "partisan" edge, particularly on those of us "who make a living by practicing one of the liberal arts . . . [and] who must occasionally wonder to what end [we] do so" (Patterson, *Pastoral* 10). Patterson, for example, acknowledges that her work on pastoral theory depends upon "the *otium* of a paid sabbatical" (*Pastoral* 331). The question is this: does writing such as Patterson's, accomplished "from a protected position, with the help of a Guggenheim Fellowship and other institutional supports," lead eventually if not all too easily to the self-serving and quietist conclusion that, concerning the role and responsibilities of intellectuals in a democratic society, "we cannot all do everything" (*Pastoral* 16, 17)?

As I have been arguing throughout this book, the answer to that question is "yes." In *Shakespeare's America, America's Shakespeare*, Bristol observes, correctly in my view, that "traditional humanist scholarship" (16) is "conservative rather than critical" not just because of its intellectual assumptions—ahistoricism, the moral value of beauty, and the like—but also because of its institutional location: "humanism has made an historical commitment to large-scale, centralized agencies of organized power *which it knows to be inimical to its deepest interests*" (22). Contemporary literary criticism does not share those intellectual assumptions— neither Patterson nor Montrose is a traditional humanist scholar—and so may be viewed as different from traditional humanism, and even perhaps as an improvement on it. But contemporary literary criticism does occupy the same institutional location as did traditional humanism and, I would suggest, has made the same historical commitment: whatever its stripe, whether feminist, Marxist, queer, Derridean, postcolonial, or new historicist, contemporary literary criticism depends upon the paid sabbatical, upon fellowships funded by Guggenheims and Rockefellers, and upon the holdings of research libraries and collections created by Gettys, Folgers, or Huntingtons. And like its humanist predecessors, contemporary literary criticism makes "this unhappy commitment," as argued in the previous chapter, to avoid the threat of a worse fate—being overwhelmed by "a popular element, a radical and levelling collective will that poses a constant threat to [its] project" (Bristol, *America* 22).

It is for reasons like these, and complicated views of history and power notwithstanding, that Simon Schama can conclude that "the greenwood generally votes conservative" (141). It is for reasons like these that I wonder what we are doing—Shakespeareans and non-Shakespeareans alike, tourists as well as residents—in the postmodern forest, in the woods outside Ashland. To ask such a question, to focus on "the human figures of pastoral" (Alpers 37) and thus on time, history, and politics, is to prompt a desire for social and environmental justice,[5] which in turn prompts consideration of the "crucial differences *among* humans and the complex cultural and historical reasons why different peoples may feel very differently about the meaning of wilderness" and nature (Cronon 45).

Some people who live in Ashland also have begun to wonder what we are doing in the woods outside their town and whether Shakespeare can contribute to social and environmental justice there. According to Beth Quinn, correspondent for *The Oregonian,* a protest erupted in September 1999 over the OSF's plan to build a new theater by moving Carpenter Hall, a historic building, to another part of town. Some in town complained about the high-handed way the Festival announced the project—one critic called the OSF a "medieval kingdom" that brooks no dissent. Others complained about labor practices at the Festival, suggesting that the OSF—a nonunion shop—does not pay its workers, especially its technicians, a living wage. But most people objected to the likelihood of yet more growth in the town, which now boasts almost 20,000 residents—an increase of 18 percent in the 1990s alone—but also 55 bed-and-breakfast inns, 68 restaurants, and, as Ashland resident Michael Sanford put it, dozens of "chichi stores . . . selling to the tourists." Most of these are located in and around the downtown that, according to Sanford, used to house "honest businesses like groceries and gas stations and department stores." Says Ashland Councilman Don Laws, "There is the fear that Shakespeare is just getting too large." Says Festival Executive Director Paul Nicholson, such fears are unavoidable "when you get a major organization in a small town. It's like General Motors in Flint, Michigan."

Shakespeare *is* living large in Ashland, and from the point of view of this writer, Nicholson's comparison of the OSF to General Motors is telling. If it is the case that some people are and will be losers in processes of fundamental environmental, economic, and cultural change, then in Ashland the losers have not been the Shakespeareans, just as in Flint, the losers have not been the stockholders of General Motors. Even the tempest over Carpenter Hall merely forced the OSF to come up with a new plan for expansion, and, Quinn reports, as of October 1999, the Festival was poised to break ground for the new theater toward the end of the 2000 season, having allayed the town's fears about growth.

Of course, the rapid growth of the OSF—three new theaters in about thirty years—correlates well with growth in Oregon more generally, including successive waves of migration from California (and elsewhere) to the state. In the late 1960s and early 1970s, these migrants were hippies and other young people—"back to the landers"—and then, beginning in the late 1970s and continuing into the 1990s, they were retirees and middle-aged urban and suburban professionals, the "equity migrants." But the OSF's growth also correlates well with the rise of environmentalism. As former artistic director Woronicz suggests, in Ashland as in Oregon, what is allowed to disturb the natural environment is the result of careful planning—a Prospero-like exercise of energy, power, and imagination. And as in *The Tempest,* planning in Oregon works for the planners, despite the occasional outcry from those subject to it—"the foul conspiracy of the beast Caliban" or of those who desire, say, a living wage and the opportunity to shop in their own downtown (4.1.139–140).

In Oregon, modern land-use planning dates from 1973, with the establishment by the Oregon Legislature of the Land Conservation and Development Corporation (LCDC) and thus of an innovative system intended to yoke—and some would say, to subordinate—planning on the local level to that on the state level: the state would establish overall policy goals and provide "oversight to ensure local government compliance with the goals. City and county governments would conduct planning studies and prepare, adopt, and administer comprehensive plans and zoning ordinances" (J. Pease 163). Since then, Oregon's collaborative system has been lauded as well as criticized, and the details of its ongoing development "have been studied, copied, modified, and sometimes rejected as Florida, Maine, New Jersey, Georgia, and other states have considered 'second generation' systems of state planning" (Abbott, Howe, and Adler ix). A concern with Oregon's experience in land-use planning is not, however, merely arcane. Because "urban sprawl" is slotted by some, particularly Vice President Al Gore, as a winning political issue, not just scholars and policy wonks but everyone has an interest in assessing Oregon's twenty-five-year experience in land-use planning. Recognizing that interest is especially important because in this case the relationship between basic (social) science research and policymaking appears to be quite weak. As a recent article in the *Chronicle of Higher Education* concludes, we really do not know whether sprawl actually causes the problems it is alleged to cause—increased pollution, a decreased sense of community, even road rage. According to the *Chronicle,* scholars in the field, including many of those who support planning efforts such as Oregon's, admit that "much of the research on land use simply isn't very good. . . . [A] lot of studies lack methodological rigor and often fail to tease out complex variables." Much planning research, says urban and regional planner Randall Crane, is "driven more by values than by traditional scholarship" (D. W. Miller A16).

One might be led to ask, "Whose values?" But for now it is more important to note that, in addition to many successes, one significant, largely unpublicized, and I would argue, negative effect[6] of Oregon's statewide planning has been the gentrification of the rural landscape, the "progressive exclusion of lower-income and blue- and pink-collar people from the land and their replacement with a much higher income group" (B. Brown 17). Contrary to popular perception, say that of a politically left professor of English residing in a city on the east coast, land-use policy in Oregon is not limited to restricting urban development (which has led, not surprisingly, to handsome financial benefits for developers and urban property owners) or to the use of national, state, or private forests. Oregon's policy extends to rural development and use as well. Nor is it intended to promote exclusively the goals of environmentalism; large-scale commercial agriculture, with its dependence on chemicals and mechanization, is one of the principle beneficiaries of Oregon's planning system. In fact, among the assumptions grounding the 1973 legislation are that small-scale or part-time agriculture (that is, resulting in less than forty thousand dollars in annual gross sales) is detrimental to commercial agricultural production, and that so, too, are nonfarm housing units and thus residents in agricultural areas. Nonfarm residents, it was argued, create tension and are sources of conflict for commercial farmers (J. Pease 167).

As a result of statewide planning in Oregon, reports Gerald Kendall, even a "simple inquiry such as 'can I place a mobile home on my property?' becomes tedious for all parties concerned" (40). Also as a result, local cynics begin to "wonder if keeping people out of the countryside is not really what Oregon land-use regulation is all about" (Leeman 54). For working-class families fortunate enough to own their own land, the latter indeed can seem to be the goal of planning. Certainly, tediousness is the least of these laws' possible effects. Already these families are squeezed by unemployment; by steeply rising property taxes (related to increased property values brought on by restrictive land-use policy itself as well as purchases by the aforementioned "equity migrants"); and by the elimination of a semi-informal economy (hunting and gathering in local woods, like development almost anywhere, is not appropriate to rationalized land use). To find they must wrangle in addition with the various land commissions—over, say, the placement of a building or the sale of a parcel of land—can become the last financial straw for them. It can force them off of their land and into cities and onto welfare, or into a semipermanent nomadic status, moving via trailer or van from one campsite to another. Throughout the Pacific Northwest, in areas where the official unemployment rate often has exceeded 20 percent and the poverty rate often has approached that level, the displaced are visible in the cities and, ironically, in state and national parks: says one local, "we're turning into turtles, carrying our house on our back" (Raphael 265).

Of course, accurate estimates of the numbers of people in the region who have lost their jobs in woods work are difficult to obtain; accurate estimates are unavailable of those who in addition have lost their property or dwellings and been forced to move. Estimates vary widely of even the cost in jobs since the early 1990s to protect spotted owl habitat, since both environmentalists and logging interests exaggerate the figures: economic consultants for the environmentalists claim almost no jobs have been lost, while the timber industry's consultants counter that the number is closer to one hundred thousand (Dietrich 283). More objective estimates suggest numbers between fifteen thousand and thirty-five thousand (M. Carroll 58–64; Raphael 249), but it should be emphasized that job loss in woods work is by no means only associated with environmentalists' efforts to protect old growth. Notoriously cyclical, subject to economic boom and bust, opportunities in woods work have been reduced as well by industrial restructuring and by technological change. New logging equipment is safer and lighter on both the land and the logger, who can snap off a tree with "barely perceptible manipulations of joystick and push button," and it also allows a couple of loggers to do the work of eight or ten men (L. Cohen 122). Total job loss in the region, therefore, is considerably higher than those reported in the debates over the fates of spotted owl habitat and old-growth forests.

By whatever measure, job loss in the region is significant, and is caused by several economic, cultural, and legal forces. Therefore, whatever estimate of the numbers one chooses to accept—thirty thousand? forty thousand?—it is clear that those who are displaced from the land as well as their jobs must be smaller, since a fair number of people manage to stitch together a viable style of life or, perhaps more accurately, a viable income. Recent sociological research on displaced timber workers in Idaho, Washington, Oregon, and California supports earlier journalistic reports, suggesting that displaced workers remain strongly attached to the land, their families, and their communities, determined to discover "ways of remaining connected . . . despite limited local [economic] opportunities (Williams and Sturtevant 2). One worker, interviewed by Matthew S. Carroll, "expressed concisely a sentiment held by many: 'Personally, I'd rather starve to death here and live off elk meat rather than participate in any degrading plans to move me around and change my culture and my life'" (148). Of course, the stubbornness of these workers, willing to accept lower and lower standards of living to remain in their communities, makes the failure to do so, the wrenching decision to leave, even more traumatic. Job loss and subsequent migration "have devastated the social landscape in the Pacific Northwest," ripping apart the small towns dominated for generations by a mill or wood products factory (Raphael 247).

Yet rather than treat this displacement as a process of gentrification, as a land grab establishing the forest not just as a playground for an elite who can "afford to relocate to what is a notoriously high-price, high-unemployment area" (B. Brown 246) but also as a place of "substantial" economic inequality (Sturtevant 5),[7] environmentalists and others treat displacement as the "personal misfortune" of workers put out of work by an unimpeachable need to protect the environment (B. Brown 246). The displaced are a problem to be solved by a state agency, and while doubtless the (upper) middle-class professionals employed to retrain displaced workers are realistic and sympathetic people, these professionals "share few social or cultural perceptions or experiences with the people they are mandated to serve" (B. Brown 251).

They do not understand, for example, that a job is not a job, and seem bewildered when former loggers or millworkers resent the opportunities offered to them by economic diversification planning agencies: government-funded retraining programs for work outside the timber industry, or low-pay and low-status jobs such as tram drivers or hotel maids or restaurant busboys supplying the needs of upper-middle-class eco- or cultural tourists. In such service work, confides a displaced worker from southern Oregon, there is "no pride in what you do to support your family, it is only a paycheck" (Williams and Sturtevant 8). Yet service work is really the only option: Kevin Williams and Victoria Sturtevant report that when they, as interviewers, brought up retraining programs, most of their informants responded with a laugh. More than ten years after the timber wars began, and more than five years after the implementation of the federal government's Northwest Forest Plan, displaced timber workers have "little knowledge of people succeeding after participating in [formal retraining] programs" (Williams and Sturtevant 9).

The professionals overseeing these efforts to assist the displaced do not understand that for working people in the Pacific Northwest, the gentrification of their communities is not an unintended consequence of protecting the environment. Rather, from their point of view, protecting the environment is a strategy of gentrification, a sign of the upper middle class's ability to move in and take over. Nor finally, do these professionals understand that workers feel caught in a crossfire between aggressive and competing elites. For them there is little difference between the environmentalists, the government, and the timber companies: all "represent people with more education, money, and powerful connections who would impose their will on the local working-class community, even when their lives might be torn apart by the consequences" (B. Brown 248). This judgment is underscored in Williams and Sturtevant's more recent research: "All participants strongly agreed that they have [been] and are being done in by powerful strangers who lacked the courage to know about the lives and forests their policies were transforming" (13).

Doubtless the powerlessness of timber workers and their families is overdetermined, and a careful teasing out of even some of the causes is beyond the scope of this chapter. But as argued in chapter 1, critical to subordinate groups' successful entry into power is a receptiveness to their claims by privileged groups, a receptiveness that privileged groups have not offered the working class in well over thirty years. Thus, when dissident Earth First! activist Judi Bari attributes to an "utter lack of class consciousness" the inability of environmental groups to enlist woods workers as allies (14), I wonder if such an explanation doesn't beg the question, particularly the question of why (upper) middle-class activists lack class consciousness. It cannot be that they lack knowledge: the (upper) middle class *chooses* to ignore the claims of class, and to privilege other claims instead.

For example, in 1987, in a gruesome incident that captured public attention and even that of *60 Minutes,* a millworker was almost decapitated by a sawblade shattered by a spiked tree:

Because the saw hit the nail square-on, there was . . . no warning sound. . . . The next thing he knew, [lifelong Mendocino County, California, resident and second-generation woods worker George Alexander] was lying on the floor covered with his own blood. . . . A 12-foot section of the huge sawblade had broken off and hit George in the throat and face, ripping through his face mask and cutting into his jugular vein. His jaw was broken in five places and a dozen teeth were knocked out. The blade was wrapped around him, and his co-workers had to blowtorch it off while they tried to keep him from bleeding to death. "The saw hit me flat," said George. "If it had hit me with the teeth I'd be dead. I'm only here because my friend Rick Phillips held my veins together in the hour before the ambulance came." (Bari 266–67)

Yet Earth First! cofounders saw fit to emphasize the plight of the trees rather than the plight of this worker: said Dave Foreman, "I think it's unfortunate that somebody got hurt, but you know I quite honestly am more concerned about old-growth forests, spotted owls and wolverines and salmon—and nobody is forcing people to cut those trees" (Bari 268).

Of course, Earth First! is among the most radical of environmentalist groups, driven by a wilderness program that, according to Timothy W. Luke, "clearly grows out of game management science," considers human beings as "one more 'natural population' that has exceeded the carrying capacity of its range," and thus "pardon[s] no one for continual complicity in nature's destruction, including native peoples, women, racial minorities, or ordinary workers" (33, 43). But moderate environmentalists also generally fail to consider the claims and the needs of the working class, even when these moderates shrink from the apocalyptic vision of Earth First!—the never fully articulated conclusion that "if humans are *the* problem, then killing most of them would be *the* solution" (Luke 42). In 1996, for example, when environmental groups like Friends of the Los Angeles River (FoLAR) sought to bulldoze Los Angeles County's massive flood control system and to replace it with, in D. J. Waldie's only slightly incredulous words, "a completely natural river," the claims of the twenty thousand people who would be displaced from their homes by such a project were ignored, as were those of the several hundred thousand working-class people who live in that river's enormous natural flood plain, the flood plain of a river that knows no bounds (116).

Environmentalists are not the only activists among the (upper) middle class who choose to ignore the claims of class. All too often, as Michael Tomasky reports, when "you express concern for workers, you are challenged:

what about people on welfare?" (12). Or what about immigrants? Or people with AIDS? Or the rain forests in Brazil, Belize, or Indonesia? Or the health and safety of laboratory animals? What is it, one is moved to ask, that makes immigrants, welfare recipients, people with AIDS, or mice, salmon, and spotted owls deserving of our attention but not a middle-aged ex-coalminer or ex-logger who, beat up and used up after years of work in a mine or forest, now makes six dollars per hour, if he or she even holds a job?[8] While the motivation behind such decisions is complex, and while I am, in fact, inclined to think highly of the motives of the (upper) middle class, agreeing with Gordon MacInnes that, for the most part, they have been "wrong for all the right reasons," I would like to suggest that the (upper) middle class writes off workers primarily for a simple reason: workers are either irrelevant to or opposed to the battles being waged.

As pointed out in chapter 1, it was in the 1960s, according to Ohmann, that the state became the "arena of struggle over entitlements" as "blacks, women, Latinos, etc." were fixed as "social categories . . . by whose fortunes the legitimacy of the social order would in part be measured" ("PC" 15). From this statement, two inferences may be made. First, workers are not part of Ohmann's "etc.," not a social category by whose fortunes the legitimacy of the social order is to be judged. Second, if the state is the "arena of struggle," then to succeed there it is necessary to control a political party, and as noted in chapter 4, the post-1968 reform of the Democratic Party achieved precisely that goal, shifting power in the name of fairness and representation to a well-educated and well-to-do elite, in particular to the left-liberal followers of George McGovern, who chaired the committee that proposed the reforms. Politics is a heavily mediated formation, professionalized and elitist, and thus increasingly offers little opportunity to the amateur or the citizen; politics at all levels is populated in disproportionate numbers by the well educated and the well-to-do.

Success in politics requires enormous financial and intellectual resources; politics is, in other words, an arena workers are not equipped to enter, much less engage successfully. Workers are irrelevant to politics, and politics is irrelevant to workers: "disengagement from political life is a central feature of working-class culture" (Croteau 170). As environmentalist Art Downing points out, reflecting on the course of environmental activism in the Pacific Northwest, political strategies requiring intellectual savvy are like a

double-edged sword. 'Cause on the one hand, those legal, intellectual strategies can be effective. They have been very effective, and they probably will be again. On the other hand, they're like good drugs. They're addictive, and they're all about control. And they put the control in the hands of people who are very intellectual. Who'll go right into their heads and deal with things in their heads. Which is unfortunate for all the people who don't work that way. And it's also unfortunate for movements, because very often the legal strategies wear out. (Interviewed by B. Brown 274)

That politics has become professionalized—or in Downing's words intellectualized—is "unfortunate" because, of course, the result of professionalization is that "all the people who don't work that way" are effectively excluded from participation in politics, from getting their interests recognized: democracy is demeaned.

Evidence suggests that such judgments are not merely paranoid. In what is perhaps only the most relevant example, consider that in 1974, Oregon's LCDC went to the people for help in drafting statewide goals for land use. LCDC's "Statewide Planning Goals and Guidelines" assert that "the 19 goals . . . were adopted after *extensive* citizen involvement in public workshops and hearings" (Leonard 141; emphasis added). Yet the commission's "People and the Land" workshops were dominated by members of the upper middle class: 52 percent of the workshoppers held bachelor's or postgraduate degrees, in contrast to about 12 percent of Oregon's population; and workshoppers' median family income was 27 percent higher than the median family income for the state (Petroff 13). Vic Petroff reports that fewer than three thousand Oregonians, "about .15% of the state's total population," participated in the first round of workshops, and about the same number (twenty-five hundred) participated in the second round (13, 15).

As a result of this biased representation, this exclusivity in the workshops, goals important to poor and working-class people, such as those concerning energy, housing, and freeway transportation, were eliminated or weakened in scope. For example, the goal for housing originally read: "Decent, safe, and sanitary housing and neighborhood environments shall be available to all people in the state at a cost that can be afforded" (Petroff 15). The goal as adopted by the LCDC reads: "Buildable lands for residential use shall be inventoried and plans shall encourage the availability of adequate numbers of housing units at price ranges and rent levels which are commensurate with the financial capabilities of Oregon households and allow for flexibility of housing location, type and density. *Buildable Lands* refers to lands in urban and urbanizable areas that are suitable, available and necessary for residential use" (Leonard 152–53). Note the changes in the latter: the emphasis on rentals; the restriction of residential use to urban and urbanizable areas; and the hedges "shall encourage" and "adequate numbers" and "commensurate with the financial capabilities of Oregon households." Note, too, that the goal as adopted contains more than twice as many words as the proposed goal, and four times as many three- and four-syllable words.

As a solution to such political exclusion, the (upper) middle class offers education. If the working class is excluded from politics because they do not have the skills or experience to participate, then they must be educated and thereby gain the needed skills and experience. Of course, as argued throughout this book, only a small percentage of the public can ever become well-educated persons: most people living in the United States are and will continue to be poorly educated and working class. One must ask, therefore, why the (upper) middle class emphasizes education to help people surmount barriers to political participation instead of, say, the elimination of the barriers, as in reducing the presence and power within politics of professionals such as lawyers, accountants, fund-raisers, media consultants, and the like, or as in making it easier for workers to vote by holding elections on Sundays or by making the exercise of the franchise an obligation.

I suggest that this solution offers two significant benefits. First, by so educating working-class people, one greatly reduces the possibility that they will continue to hold social and cultural opinions that from the point of view of liberal elites are conservative or retrograde: as pointed out in chapter 1, the best predictor of social and cultural liberalism is high levels of education (Brint 86–87, 97–103; Croteau 195–96; Riesman and Glazer 125–26). Second, the attempt at education, which acknowledges the distress of the excluded and offers to some the opportunity of inclusion, legitimates a second course of action, which is punishment for those who do not take well to education and yet continue to press their political claims from the other side of the fence, those who behave as if voice were not dependent on educational and class attainment but merely on citizenship. Thus, when working-class people disagree with the agendas of the (upper) middle class or resist top-down impositions such as busing and affirmative action or the elimination of all extraction in federal or even private forests, their resistance is dismissed and they are demonized as racists or as rapists of the earth, moves that, as a number of writers observe, simply do "not do justice to the complexity of the issue(s)" involved (Croteau 216; Edsall and Edsall; MacInnes; Sleeper; and Tomasky).

Social scientists describe this demonization as "moral exclusion." Like opponents of busing, rapists of the earth are deemed to be "non-entities, expendable, or undeserving; consequently, harming them appears acceptable, appropriate, or just" (Opotow 1). Moral exclusion is what makes "redneck jokes . . . the last acceptable ethnic slurs in 'polite' society" (Roskelly 293) and moral exclusion is what allows one to open up a copy of *River Styx* and read a poem by Antler entitled "Job Replacement for Loggers of Old Growth" (28–29). *River Styx* is not the *Earth First! Journal,* nor is it slapped together by a bunch of students in an MFA program. It is glossy and well funded and important—elite and influential writers of a variety of races, genders, and sexualities grace its pages, writers like Ishmael Reed, Gary Snyder, William Gass, Howard Nemerov, Mona Van Duyn, Adrienne Rich, Toni Morrison, Derek Walcott, Rita Dove, and Diane Wakowski. And the people who publish *River Styx* in St. Louis, Missouri, sponsor readings in pleasant surroundings for people with lots of money or other kinds of capital—people like you and me. Perhaps Antler, who is one of the most popular poets in the United States, according to *Writer's Chronicle,* read "Job Replacement for Loggers of Old Growth" at such a gathering.

In doing so, Antler would have read a list of twenty-four replacement jobs for loggers. It is a poem that uses much pastoral imagery and even focuses on the human figure in the forest, but it not a pastoral poem in Alpers's sense. Certainly, it does not bemoan the fate of the dispossessed. It is not a poem celebrating social or environmental justice. What we see instead is that in twelve jobs, loggers are given jobs that punish them for having worked as loggers. Sometimes, these jobs constitute reeducation.

In some of these jobs, loggers must meditate on their sins, while sometimes amusing or entertaining or being helpful to others. In others, they must be publicly humiliated:

> 12. Get paid twelve times as much to learn wilderness birdsongs
>   and sing them on busy citystreetcorners
>   to passersby.

Sometimes, these jobs force the loggers to fix the damage they have done:

> 4. Be paid four times as much to plant trees,
>   to re-Sequoia America, to re-White Pine, re-Chestnut,
>   re-Elm, re-Oak, re-Maple, re-Birch,
>   re-Redwood America.

In six jobs, the loggers are forced to become artists or craftspersons or intellectuals. And in three jobs, loggers are punished physically for having logged. In number 5, loggers must spike trees, thereby forcing other loggers to desist from logging or risk injury and even death. In number 11, Antler envisions the loggers killing themselves for eleven times their pay as loggers: these loggers are pitifully stupid and will do anything for money. And in number 23, Antler suggests that the loggers "Be paid twenty-three times as much for being / a state-certified boycocksucker ready / 24-hours-a-day / to service needy boyboners in the name of Ecotopia." Job number 23 is quite fantastic, but fantasies come in many forms, and in the end, since Antler speaks about jobs, one cannot help but wonder where all this money will come from. For Antler, materialism is the defining characteristic of the loggers, as the controlling device of the poem suggests: each job description begins with "be paid" or "get paid" and each offers a wage more lavish than the next. But "Job Replacement for Loggers of Old Growth" would be a more honest poem if Antler punished the loggers at a fraction of their pay: one-half, one-quarter, one-sixteenth, one-thirty-second, one-sixty-fourth, nothing, not a god-damned red cent.

Even if they do not know the social scientists' term for their demonization, displaced woods workers surely would recognize it—their moral exclusion—in a poem like Antler's (cf. Williams and Sturtevant 11–15). What we should recognize in it is first that the (upper) middle class has abandoned "faith in the mass of people to be fair and make reasonable moral judgments" (Tomasky 164); and second that this class is vitally concerned with, as Downing puts it, control: control of the environment, of college admissions, of institutions of government, of the terms by which the legitimacy of the social order will be judged.

In the Pacific Northwest, environmental battles, therefore, are less about owls or salmon or thousand-year-old trees than about the control of the land. What has occurred in the past two decades is that environmentalists have wrested control of the land from transnational timber corporations by winning the support of significant portions of state and federal government, including the judiciary. In addition to laudable efforts to protect habitat and wildlife, this transfer of power has resulted in less noted effects: the elimination of tens of thousands of well-paying working-class jobs; the transfer of rural property from the working class to the upper middle class; and the regulation of land use on both private and public lands, resulting in the elimination or severe reduction of access to the "public commons" of fishing sites, blackberry patches, and mushrooming areas. Taken together, these developments have resulted in the (forced) movement of tens of thousands of the working class into crowded and anonymous urban areas, or into semipermanent vagabondage.

This scenario is familiar to scholars of the early modern period; it describes (some of) the effects of enclosure, a word we use to signify the uneven and centuries-long process by which the open-field system of village farming was replaced by a system of independent, consolidated, and private farming. Because enclosure was, as Thirsk defines it, a "method of increasing the productivity or profitability of land" by restricting its use (4), and because enclosure resulted in the displacement of large numbers of the rural populace, it is not far-fetched to propose that the term *enclosure* be applied to the regulation of land use in the Pacific Northwest today. Indeed, today's environmentalists and the sixteenth century's enclosers—whether Crown, nobleman, gentry, or tenant farmer—justify their attempts to control the land in similar terms. Both are keen to improve the land and to prevent wasteful production; both vilify those who resist those improvements; and both are responsible for the displacement of thousands of people from the improved rural environments.

In closing this chapter, I wish to point out that the criterion by which we judge Shakespeare—that enclosure is invariably a negative—seems not to apply to twentieth-century environmentalism. For me, this inconsistency is troubling because it directly contradicts what Joan Wallach Scott calls intellectuals' "most valuable—and pleasurable—activity: thinking hard about everything, from obscure texts to our present condition" (23), in this case, broadly speaking, about what we are doing in the woods, or the complex meanings of enclosure, pastoral, environmentalism, and cultural tourism. Of course, to counter the charge that on this issue intellectuals indulge in anti-intellectual behavior, one might suggest that, say, enclosure is the wrong kind of control and that environmentalism is the right kind of control. But such a reply begs the issue in revealing only the preferences of the literary critics themselves; worse, it suggests that mass displacement and social dislocation is an acceptable consequence of the right kind of control. One might also suggest that I have no evidence that literary or cultural critics hold such views, condemning early modern enclosures while supporting and even facilitating contemporary environmentalism.

To this latter objection, I concede: I hypothesize here in suggesting that the same liberality producing a concern for those displaced in the battles over land use in early modern England does not produce a concern for those displaced in the battles over land use in late-twentieth-century America. But I make this hypothesis based on anecdotal evidence, what colleagues say to me at conferences, in airports, at dinner in trendy urban restaurants; and based on the written record, the fact that scholars of the early modern period often attempt to make the past usable, commenting on the relevance of their historical scholarship to contemporary cases of oppression or ideological misrecognition. The nod to the present has included contemporary rape trials (in Stephanie Jed's work), the Anita Hill–Clarence Thomas affair (in Linda Charnes's), and the don't ask, don't tell policy for homosexuals in the military (in Katherine Maus's). What the nod to the present has missed or avoided—until now—is the unhappy plight of those who resist, or indeed are victims of, the contemporary political and cultural judgments, or rather the nostalgia, of the scholars themselves.

The present is my Cleopatra, and in this chapter she has "nodded [me] to her" (*Antony and Cleopatra* III.vi.66). Now that I am with her, I'm not leaving. It's foolish, I know, because Octavius Caesar is out there waiting to sink this ship. But in the next chapter, my conclusion, you will look unsuccessfully for a reference to early modern England or even to Shakespeare. Still, the larger concerns of this book require me to contribute to a debate recently begun in the United States about the nature of the Left, a debate that coalesces around the aims and interests of an older "social" Left and a newer "cultural" Left and that, for me, extends as well to the nature of professional life in the university. So, I am going to do it, without Will.

CHAPTER SIX

Conclusion
Seeing Red, Seeing the Rift in the Left

I first read about it when *The Nation* arrived in my mailbox in early June 1996 and I opened it to find Katha Pollitt's column, "Pomolotov Cocktail." Or perhaps it was somewhat before that, because one of the old guard in my department, someone who thinks the theory-emperor has no clothes, doubtless slipped into our boxes a copy of Alan Sokal's own homemade bomb, published in *Lingua Franca* ("Physicist" 62). There the physicist revealed he had successfully completed "a modest (though admittedly uncontrolled) experiment: Would a leading North American journal of cultural studies—whose editorial collective includes such luminaries as Fredric Jameson and Andrew Ross—publish an article liberally salted with nonsense if (a) it sounded good and (b) it flattered the editors' ideological preconceptions?"

Of the Left himself, and motivated by an unhappiness with the form, content, and consequences of identity or cultural politics—so much "silliness emanating from the self-proclaimed Left" ("Physicist" 64)—Sokal discovered that the answer to his question was, in fact, yes. *Social Text* published "Transgressing the Boundaries: Toward a Transformative Hermeneutics of Quantum Gravity," an article written so that "any competent physicist or mathematician (or undergraduate physics or math major) would realize that it is a spoof," and *Social Text* did so without "bothering to consult anyone knowledgeable in the subject" ("Physicist" 63).

For the next month or so, the Sokal affair was big news, as journalists and academics bristled and strutted while defending and mocking *Social Text*.[1] But as with all such media eruptions, this one died down rather quickly, and by the end of 1997, in an essay also published in *Social Text*, Judith Butler could refer to it simply as "the hoax of last year" (266). Quietly referred to or not, however, the challenge of the Sokal affair lingers, because it is a symptom of a larger problem: a rift in the Left, between an older Left focused on class and a newer Left focused on culture. This rift is the result of what, in *Justice Interruptus*, her collection of essays published in 1997, Nancy Fraser calls a "decoupling of cultural politics from social politics, and the relative eclipse of the latter by the former" (2).

In this chapter, for convenience and simplicity, I will refer to a social Left that pursues class politics (heirs or perhaps remnants of the old Left) and to a cultural Left that pursues cultural politics (heirs of the New Left). But other terms have been offered by other writers: Richard Rorty, for example, refers to a "reformist" Left and a "cultural" Left, academic heirs of the New Left (43, 76); Stanley Aronowitz refers at times to "welfare state leftism" and "cultural radicalism" and at other times to the economic-justice Left and the cultural Left (*Death* 16–17, 109); and Todd Gitlin refuses to acknowledge any historical relationship between the old Left and the new Left, since the Left now is not a Left but a fragmented, "ragtag party" that "speaks for no movement" and "fails to generate an emotional tide" (*Dreams* 103; Aronowitz, *Death* 90). In any case, regardless of the historical and ideological nuances captured in the many terms offered to describe the rift in the Left, it is at least safe to say that by now we all know there is one.

Butler's essay for *Social Text* attacks unnamed promoters of a "neoconservatism within the Left" who seek "the redomestication and resubordination of . . . differences" in the name of a "unity" that "prioritize[s] a racially cleansed notion of class" (276, 269, 268). Strong stuff, this, even incendiary; but in the last year or two, Butler claims, these left neoconservatives have become increasingly bold in relegating "new social movements to the sphere of the cultural" and in demonizing them "as being preoccupied with what is called the 'merely' cultural" and with a cultural politics that is "factionalizing, identitarian, and particularistic" (265). Among these unnamed on the left, however, sits one named target, Nancy Fraser, whose views in *Justice,* Butler acknowledges, "are in no way orthodox" but nevertheless, she claims, reproduce "the division that locates certain oppressions as part of political economy and relegates others to the exclusively cultural sphere" (270).

It is not my aim here to judge the accuracy of Butler's claims, although I will note again that theoretical and empirical work on the new social movements (NSMs) does suggest that they are "factionalizing, identitarian, and particularistic."[2] Differences between NSMs and older class or workers' movements are significant: NSMs aim not to redesign the state but to work within it and indeed to use it to improve the status of particular groups—women, people of color, homosexuals—or to advance a particular political cause, the peace movement or environmentalism, for example. As argued in chapters 2, 4, and 5, NSMs advance these causes via institutions available primarily to the highly educated, such as the courts, the media, and increasingly the political parties themselves.

While it is easy to agree with Butler that the old social Left's claim to universalism was dubious at best, it would also seem that the inclusiveness or exclusiveness of a movement is a matter of degree, as Barry Barnes acknowledges: unlike the NSMs (with the possible exception of feminism), the class-based movements of the past held "large aims beneficial to majorities in their host populations" such as the extension of the franchise, the right to organize as workers, or the extension of equal protection under the law (161). Further, although "it would be excessive to claim that there is some mathematical law of inverse proportion between social justice and cultural radicalism" (Aronowitz, *Death* 4), research in Europe suggests that "a zero-sum relationship" does exist between the saliency of the concerns of the social Left and the "corresponding capacity of the new social movements to articulate new issues" (Kriesi et al. 25). Where the old social Left is strong, the new cultural Left is weak and vice versa. What this "strong inverse relationship" (240) suggests, however, is not simply that in certain instances, say in Germany or the Netherlands, we have moved in a nicely progressive way beyond class conflict. Class remains central to left politics not because the cultural Left speaks for or to any given class but because the cultural Left is an expression of a given class, namely, of the professional middle or New Class. As Croteau remarks, the initiatives of the cultural Left "clearly [are] conducted *by* a class": in both the United States and Europe, the NSMs are rooted strongly in a (upper) middle-class base (31, 32; Brint 199–200).

In any case, and notwithstanding these comments on NSMs, Fraser does not need me to defend her. Her response to Butler in *Social Text* does the job well. And anyone who has read the chapters of *Justice* to which Butler refers can see that Butler misreads her, mistaking, as Fraser puts it in *Social Text*, "what is actually a quasi-Weberian dualism of status and class for an orthodox Marxian economistic monism" (281). Such a misreading could have occurred for many reasons, but I suspect two, principally. First, Butler accurately notices that some on the Left are making totalizing noises, are trying to throw the identity politics baby out with the bath. And second—and more important to my argument here—Butler may not like the political implications of Fraser's argument.

When the topic of class comes up, Butler sees only red: an orthodox Marxism seeking to reestablish hegemony. And seeing red makes her angry: have the historical reasons for the emergence of new social movements, of the cultural Left, been forgotten so quickly? As Fraser puts it in *Justice*, these "movements arose in the first place precisely to protest the disguised particularism—the masculinism, the white-Anglo ethnocentrism, the heterosexism—lurking behind what parades as universal" (5). "Marxism," observes NSM theorist Carl Boggs, "largely failed to confront the problem of domination in its multiple forms" (59). Richard Rorty is more succinct and casts fault more generally: "most of the direct beneficiaries of [the social Left's] initiatives were white males" (75).[3]

But as I argue throughout this book, seeing red when the topic of class comes up *is* the problem. Seeing red—Butler's willingness to link Fraser with "neoconservative Marxisms" (268)—allows Butler to divert attention from the political and theoretical implications of Fraser's argument, which is to say that the claims of class politics are incommensurable with the claims of identity politics: speaking analytically and theoretically, "redistributive remedies for political-economic injustice always dedifferentiate social groups [and] recognition remedies for cultural-valuational injustice always enhance social group differentiation" (*Justice* 23). Speaking practically or empirically, this is to say that in the thirty years since the Left has pursued the politics of race and gender, the admirable and important gains made there have been accompanied by serious losses in the politics of class: as emphasized in chapters 2 and 5, the United States, under a Democratic president, developed the most unequal distribution of income of any advanced industrial society, and it is increasingly difficult, if not impossible, for workers in the United States who do not hold a college degree—and these are the vast majority of workers—to earn enough money to support a family or what used to be called a middle-class lifestyle.

Rorty acknowledges this same point, noting that "the dark side to the success story [of] the post-Sixties cultural Left" is that "during the same period in which socially accepted sadism has steadily diminished, economic inequality has steadily increased" (83). Yet unlike Rorty, who cheerfully concludes that the rift in the Left is a matter of focus and attitude, of getting it together to concentrate simultaneously on problems of sadism and economic inequality (83), Fraser and Butler and I, as well as Gitlin and Aronowitz, acknowledge the problem to be bigger, more difficult than that.

In addition to the hot potato of having to change policies and the distribution of governmental largesse, a solution would require that both the cultural Left and the social Left stop seeing red when the topic of class comes up. Class inequality, as argued throughout this book, need not and should not be described in reductive economic terms. Recognizing the cultural as well as economic dimensions of class difference, however, would require both the cultural Left and the social Left to consider the sources and effects of the power of people like ourselves. When we think about class and only see red, we free ourselves from that difficult and disturbing task. Given all that, it is perhaps not surprising that Butler answers Fraser's concern for class politics by dismissing it, linking it with an unacceptable, hegemonic, and retrograde Marxism; or that, more recently, David Palumbo-Liu answers Rorty's and Gitlin's concern by demonizing them—using ad hominem attack, misrepresentations of their arguments, and a polarizing and indeed moralizing framework for analysis.

According to Palumbo-Liu, these are "heterosexual, white, middle-class male progressives" who have been squeezed out of "the American conversation" and who, in "deep discomfort," are now attempting to recoup their positions by using "'class' as a tool to deflate the claims of race, sexuality, gender, and so on" (51). Palumbo-Liu insists that Gitlin's and Rorty's "distortions and half-truths are attributable" to their personal histories, their nostalgic reveries about one or another version of the Left (45–46). And, like Butler, he claims that what these writers want to do is reassert "the priority of the economic" (45). Yet neither Rorty and Gitlin does so, and neither tries to "deflate" the claims of race and gender. Rorty in particular celebrates the achievements of the cultural Left (75–83). If Rorty and Gitlin give priority to anything, it is to the political, and to the practical realities associated with it, as Gitlin argues: "a Left that was serious about winning political power . . . would take it as elementary to reduce friction among white men, blacks, white women, and Hispanics" (*Dreams* 234).

In this, Rorty and Gitlin recall many liberals of the 1950s and 1960s, who anticipated the political consequences of the New Left's rejection of the working class but were powerless to do much more than to encourage "a slow regathering of forces among the liberal-labor-left in the United States," a regathering that would, in their vision, merge or address equally the economic concerns of workers and the moral concerns of the young, as Irving Howe put it in 1970 ("Introduction" 14–15). I cannot help but wonder what Howe would make of Palumbo-Liu's rejection of Rorty and Gitlin: is thirty years not slow enough for a slow regathering? Or would Howe now suspect that this is an interested rejection? The partiality and defensiveness in Palumbo-Liu's discussion suggest as much: the mere idea of a regathered "liberal-labor-left" storm, of a political coalition among working-class peoples of both genders and all colors, gives Palumbo-Liu the kind of "deep discomfort" he attributes to Rorty and Gitlin. It does so because such a (re)turn to class politics threatens his and the cultural Left's power.

Strategies like Butler's or Palumbo-Liu's can be effective, for within the realm of ideology, "an argument prevails when its opponents are coerced into being quiet" (Collins, *Conflict* 472). Within the hierarchical and status-driven realm of the university, this coercion can affect the young, especially. Consider, for example, the 1997 collection *White Trash: Race and Class in America,* edited by two graduate students in literature at Berkeley, Matt Wray and Annalee Newitz. Newitz and Wray's introduction is significant in that it could have been written only by people of their intellectual generation: the editors were twenty-eight and thirty-three, respectively, at the time of publication. Starting points for them are multiculturalism and whiteness studies, and their goals are to contest what they call "vulgar multiculturalist assumption[s]" such as, for example, that "whiteness must always equal terror and racism" or that "whiteness can only be assimilated into a multicultural society once it is associated with victimhood" (5, 6). Admirable goals these, which to achieve requires some frank talk about class, but for Newitz and Wray to do so, they must talk about race, sneaking Sally through the alley, so to speak. They assay an analogy—"a white trash position vis-à-vis whiteness might be compared to a 'racial minority' position vis-à-vis whiteness"—in order to make, tentatively, the obvious point that there exist "certain commonalities between oppressed whites and oppressed racial groups" (5).

As a result, it should not surprise (though it does) that in a collection professing to talk about class in the United States, Karl Marx is cited but twice, once more than Groucho but less than half as often as Roseanne or John Wayne Bobbitt. I mean no disrespect to the editors, but I suspect that only persons having to discover class consciousness on their own could celebrate such insights about whiteness, and only persons whose graduate education began in, say, the last fifteen years or so could be in such a position: certainly, Rorty—proud member of the old social Left—would be shocked to learn that "whiteness is . . . rarely connected to poverty in the U.S. imaginary" (8). Still, this is not (only) a personal failing on the editors' part, for Newitz and Wray exemplify a disciplinary amnesia or forgetfulness that seems endemic to contemporary scholarship. As Gans argues, a bibliography that stretches only two decades into the past is essential for scholars who need to be not only up-to-date and original but also productive: "forgetting the past is functional for increasing (artificially to be sure) the number of original findings, and the number of articles and books that can be produced" (*Sense* 296).[4]

What all of this suggests is that the structure of contemporary scholarship, combined with the hegemony of the cultural Left, with its focus on race and gender, has left young scholars without the practical or theoretical tools necessary to address the subject of class or, in what amounts to the same task, to contest their elders. Circumscribed by requirements of what Guillory calls "preprofessionalism" ("Students" 92) and by the theoretical choices of their professors—Bakhtin, Foucault, and Jameson are the featured theorists of this volume, with, thankfully, Bourdieu as well—Newitz and Wray work very hard to reinvent the wheel, concluding with evident pride what is a simple and basic point in the non-Marxian sociological literature on stratification, that "class actually cuts across race lines" (8).

Of course, as argued throughout this book and particularly in chapters 1 and 3, an ignorance of the long tradition of work in what most Marxists mostly dismiss as "bourgeois sociology" arguably accounts for the current crisis about whether class is a useful concept for literary and cultural study (as well as for a volume like *White Trash* that addresses class without attending to theoretical work on it). One might hypothesize, in fact, that had the Left been reading outside as well as inside the Marxian tradition, it would not have been vulnerable in the 1960s to attack on the issues of race and gender. As H. H. Gerth and C. Wright Mills pointed out in 1946 in introducing their famous translation of Weber, "by making this sharp distinction between *class* and *status,* and by differentiating between types of classes and types of status groups, Weber is able to refine the problems of stratification to an extent which thus far has not been surpassed" (69). And these refinements still have not been surpassed, according to Collins: Weber's "diversifying of the Marxian class scheme with status groups . . . gives the theoretical potential for treating ethnicity and sex, problems that have remained intractable from the Marxian viewpoint" (*Theory* 6).

The hypothesis offered in the previous paragraph is not correct, however: in the 1950s, some on the left were reading theorists other than Marx and taking them seriously. But these thinkers were doomed to be rejected by a younger generation of scholars, and not just because scholarly "generations seem almost inherently reluctant to acknowledge the utility of past generations," as Cans paraphrases Karl Mannheim's argument of 1927 (*Sense* 296–97). The break in the late 1950s and early 1960s between the old Left and the New Left and between the senior professors and their graduate students was fueled not just by a typical anxiety of influence but by significant cultural differences and expectations, arising out of the conditions of the 1950s: increased affluence, the cold war and the bomb, rock 'n' roll and youth culture generally, the widely perceived generation gap.[5]

For "the rebelling young scholars" working in the late 1950s, wholesale rejection describes their relationship to "the men at whose feet they have chosen to sit" (Hacker 404). The orthodoxies against which the young scholars in history and the social sciences pitched their revolt included important questions of method, particularly what Andrew Hacker called "a misplaced obsession with 'objectivity'" (406) and a problem of ideology, or perhaps more accurately, a problem of nonideology—that is, the "the cult of consensus" that emerged in American history and politics in the late 1940s and 1950s. In John Higham's account, published in 1959, this "fundamental change of direction in the exploration of the American past" offered students and the nation a "strikingly conservative" reevaluation of American history that stressed not power and conflict but continuity, "the stability of basic institutions, the toughness of the social fabric" (93, 100, 95).

In retrospect, it is not surprising that the tool used to reject this "celebration" of the American past and present was an intellectual tradition that had "been beyond the academic pale for the past twenty years" (Hacker 407). In so embracing Marx, the graduate students and their younger comrades in the New Left rejected not only the anticommunism of their professors but also the old Left's "preoccupation with the Russian question," whether pro or con (Aronowitz, *Death* 17). Less interested than their predecessors in doctrine or debate—Gitlin recalls that the old Left's "political culture was one of talmudic disputation" (*Sixties* 76)—these young radicals found in Marx historical and theoretical grounding for the kind of utopian thinking and activist encounters, for style and authenticity, being urged upon them by writers like Paul Goodman and Herbert Marcuse.

Hacker accurately guessed that this "cold war" in the graduate schools would have a profound and lasting effect on intellectual life and higher education in the United States (404, 412; Diggins 288–98). When Marxism eventually became retooled in an intellectually rigorous way, as it had to be—for "it is not that Marxism creates radicals; each new generation of radicals creates its own Marx" (Bell, paraphrasing Charles Frankel, *End* 433)—it reflected the concerns expressed by Hacker's young rebels. Focused around the work of the Frankfurt school, Georg Lukács, and especially Antonio Gramsci, and based on Marx's early philosophic manuscripts (the vast majority of which were not published in the lifetimes of either Marx or Engels and thus were implicitly repudiated by them), this retooled Marxism addressed and continues to address problems of culture, not political economy, and is thus "heretical" to the "historical" Marx (Bell, *End* 433, 425–26, 365; Gitlin, *Dreams* 94–104). And in this heretical formation, what Hacker in 1960 called Marxism without socialism (409, 412), "class" becomes easy to forget, even as it remains, residually—or emptily, in Guillory's phrase—on everyone's lips.

Also easy to forget is that the intellectual roots of the cultural Left may be traced to the work of bourgeois social scientists of the 1950s as easily as to the work of radical intellectuals in search of new agents of social change, of substitutes for those disappointing losers, the working class—"for the proletariat that failed" and betrayed their historic mission (Harrington 35; Hacker 412). In fact, in 1962 one of the consensus historians described by Higham, Richard Hofstadter, proposed the term "cultural politics" to expand upon the term "status politics," which he first used in 1955 in an essay published in *The New American Right*, a volume edited by Daniel Bell. In that volume, prominent sociologists and historians attempted to explain the phenomenon of Senator Joseph McCarthy, which seemed to defy standard political analysis based on conflict between interest groups, either sectional or economic.

The result of a faculty seminar on political behavior, particularly McCarthyism, conducted at Columbia University in 1954, *The New American Right* offered "a new framework" to understand politics, "derived from an analysis of the exhaustion of liberal and left-wing political ideology," as Bell put it in his contribution ("Politics" 4). Key to this new framework was the notion of status politics, which sociologist Seymour Martin Lipset defined as involving "political movements whose appeal is to the not uncommon resentments of individuals or groups who desire to maintain or improve their social status" ("Sources" 168) but which Hofstadter defined as "the clash of various projective rationalizations arising from status aspirations and other personal motives" ("Revolt" 43).

The New American Right caused quite a stir, as did an expanded and updated version, *The Radical Right*, when it appeared eight years later. Hofstadter, in particular, was subject to "several years of pummeling," according to Robert Collins, because his work in *The New American Right* almost coincided with the appearance of *The Age of Reform*, which won him a Pulitzer Prize and a fair amount of fame (155). Although by 1962, Hofstadter had become "disposed to regret" his "excessive emphasis" on individual psychology in understanding status politics ("Revisited" 100), he continued to use that "increasingly confused" concept in influential and highly visible work, particularly *Anti-Intellectualism in American Life*, published in 1963 and also recipient of a Pulitzer Prize, and *The Paranoid Style in American Politics*, published in 1965 (Singal 993).

Accordingly, Hofstadter never formulated a definition of the concept that could match Lipset's in explanatory power; at the same time, Hofstadter's fame may well have kept Lipset's analysis from gaining wider currency. Certainly, from the Weberian point of view described in this book, Lipset's definition of status politics—that is, "political movements whose appeal is to the not uncommon resentments of individuals or groups who desire to maintain or improve their social status" ("Sources" 168)—hits closer to the mark than does Hofstadter's "clash of various projective rationalizations." The former allows for the analysis of progressive as well as conservative or reactionary status group politics, and because it does not emphasize the irrational, it does not "have the a priori effect of discrediting any group to whom it is applied" (Potter 26). Indeed, a consistently drawn if obviously understated theme in both *The New American Right* and *The Radical Right* is that the right has no monopoly on status politics: status politics can be used for both conservative or progressive ends, and can be used well or badly by any group (in the 1955 volume, see Lipset, "Sources," and Hofstadter, "Revolt"; in the 1963 volume, see Parsons, "Postscript"; Westin; and Lipset "Decades"; see also Potter).

Given the influence of Hofstadter and the problems in both collections— for example, the suggestion that those concerned with status politics are irrational, unconscious, and vague about their demands, or that outbreaks of status politics correlate with periods of economic prosperity and outbreaks of class politics with periods of economic depression—one might argue that in this case, perhaps (inter)disciplinary amnesia was for the best. I do not think so. In addition to reasons noted by H. Gans, to which I alluded earlier in this chapter, another reason is that such amnesia itself fosters what Benjamin DeMott, in his 1988 reassessment of mid-1950s social critics, calls "the illusion of autonomy," which, as we all know, can lead in academe and elsewhere to inflated senses of personal accomplishment and importance. Especially in this day, DeMott seems to suggest, it is important to remind ourselves "of the messy, unpredictable ways in which . . . we continue to live life backward and forward in time, and can never win full release from the hand of the past" (68).

But more importantly, in this case (inter)disciplinary amnesia has kept us from easy acquaintance with a number of important hypotheses and findings offered in *The New American Right, The Radical Right*, and scores of other publications by the contributors and their peers—hypotheses and findings that, had we paid more attention to them, might have helped us avoid the situation we find ourselves in today, a situation in which, for example, a prominent left scientist finds it necessary to fool a prominent left journal in order to protest the *irrationality* of the cultural Left, the "first Left in American or European history to distrust the . . . Enlightenment" (Diggins 347, 373–83; Gitlin, *Dreams* 3–4, 210–19; Sokal, "Physicist" 63). It is a situation in which the Left engages almost exclusively in status politics (while calling it something else) and employs tactics similar to those of the McCarthyites and Birchers of *The Radical Right*. It is a Left that is separatist, resentful, antimodern, antielitist, ideological, and prone to scapegoating.

What we might have learned from Hofstadter, Bell, Riesman and Glazer, Parsons, and Lipset is what we also might have learned from Weber and what we might still learn from Fraser or this book: status groups are about maintaining and furthering the interests of the group. They are about inclusion, therefore, only under carefully bounded conditions; for the most part, they are about exclusion. Whether professors of literature, physicians, Catholics, lesbians, African Americans, the French, or members of the social register, that is their function. As such, according to Talcott Parsons in 1955, status group politics "*cuts clean across the traditional lines of distinction between 'conservatives' and 'progressives,'* especially where that tends to be defined, as it so often is, in terms of the capitalistic or moneyed interests as against those who seek to bring them under more stringent control" (*Strains,* 136). Furthermore, status group politics depends upon the achievement of a certain level of material well-being—it is a "luxury"—and involves a "drive for recognition and respectability" (Hofstadter, "Revolt" 43; Bell, "Politics" 4). Admirable goals, perhaps, but not necessarily: it depends on whether that culture deserves political recognition and whether such political recognition is a sort of zero-sum game. Certainly, status groups behave as if it were such a game: common tactics are to "convert politics into 'moral' issues," to polarize debate, and to create scapegoats, tactics that especially worried the contributors to *The New American Right,* according to Bell. Although mainly analytical, he writes, "the essays in this book . . . point to a dangerous situation. The tendency to convert issues into ideologies, to invest them with moral color and high emotional charge, invites conflicts which can only damage a society" ("Politics" 20, 27).

If all this sounds prescient, a fifty-year-old description of today's political and intellectual cultures, that is because I have been selective in my citings of this body of work; it is also because it *is* prescient. The contributors to *The New American Right* anticipate many of the complaints Butler assigns to "Left neoconservatives"; they anticipate some of my complaints in this book. Thus a focus by the Left on civil liberties and civil rights, explained David Riesman and Nathan Glazer, also in 1955, is one that "differs politically from the old New Deal causes in that it represents for many liberals and intellectuals a withdrawal from the larger statist concerns—it is a cause which is carried into personal life and into the field of culture" (75). It is, furthermore, a focus that makes intellectuals seek allies among those who share that culture, "among the rich and well-born rather than among the workingmen and farmers they had earlier courted and cared about; indeed, it tends to make them conservative, once it becomes clear that civil liberties are protected, not by majority vote (which is overwhelmingly unsympathetic), but by traditional institutions, class prerogatives, and judicial life-tenure" (78). Such a focus divides workers from intellectuals, and it does so, in addition, because workers do not have the economic capital or the cultural capital—"the practice of deference and restraint which is understood and appreciated . . . among the well-to-do and highly educated" (78)—to see these issues as meaningful. For workers these issues mean mainly sacrifice, either economically or culturally, which is not the case for intellectuals, the rich, or the well-born. Liberal intellectuals may not have liked it then, and the cultural Left may not have liked it since, but Riesman and Glazer were and are correct: "the demand for tolerance . . . cannot replace, politically, the demand of 'economic equality'" (75).

In *Anti-Intellectualism in American Life*, Hofstadter concluded that "since any alliance between intellectuals and the people is bound to be imperfect, a democratically loyal intellectual class is bound to suffer acute disappointment" (408). Hofstadter did not, perhaps could not, anticipate the extent to which "the intellectual class" would punish "the people" for being so disappointing, but he did know that it "is rare for an American intellectual to confront candidly the unresolvable conflict between the elite character of his own class and his democratic aspirations" (407–8). Since 1963, such a candid confrontation has become even more difficult to achieve, as American intellectuals have asserted ever more militantly their commitments to egalitarianism by pursuing status group politics, a strategy that benefits only themselves and a minority of those previously excluded from mainstream institutional power in the United States. Such a strategy cannot achieve an egalitarian outcome—it is, shall we say, egalitarianism in drag—and as such exemplifies either mystification or false consciousness, which may account for the contempt most of "the people" feel for it and those who pursue it.

Interestingly, although at the time most reviewers of *Anti-Intellectualism in American Life* regarded it as elitist, a judgment reinforced in 1992 by Eric Foner (602), Hofstadter accepts that in the United States, broad-based anti-intellectualism springs from "benevolent impulses" and "has often been linked to good, or at least defensible, causes," such as beliefs in God, equality, universal education, and hard work and enterprise (22–23). The relationship between the people and intellectuals is inevitability imperfect and disappointing precisely because anti-intellectualism helps to constitute, along with antielitism more generally, "the democratic institutions and egalitarian sentiments of this country" (407). Hofstadter supports neither the elimination of anti-intellectualism nor the right of intellectuals to do as they please. He worries, for instance, about the effects on intellectual life of, on the one hand, the power and wealth that flow from professionalization (34–37, 428) and, on the other hand, of the tendency to turn "alienation" into an "obligation which preconditions all . . . other obligations" (420). And he proposes that in the United States, much intellectual bad faith, as well as our many "pricks of conscience," can be traced to being elite in a democratic society: we "feel the constant necessity of justifying [our] role," a need that sets us apart from our European counterparts, who "usually take for granted the worth of what they are doing and the legitimacy of their claims on the community" (417).

To some, it may be surprising that since 1963, humanists—and perhaps literary critics in particular—have felt increased pressure to justify our role even as (or even though) we have upped our commitment to diversity and the political study of literature and culture. To me, it is not surprising and reflects that "the people" are less gullible than we think them to be. Like Fish, they know that "doing full justice to the verbal intricacy of a poem" and "inquiring into the agendas in whose service that intricacy has been put" are different tasks (*Correctness* 69). Like Fish, they know that doing the latter instead of the former within the institutional context of the university is not a radical act (*Correctness* 101). Unlike Fish, and precisely because they have experienced the "agendas" supported by the intricacies of language, I am not sure that they care whether we self-destruct by abandoning "the skills of close reading that are identified with, and give a distinctive identity to, the profession of literary studies" (*Correctness* 69).

Fish clearly does care, however, and thinks something valuable "will have passed from the earth" if no one "takes up the tools of close reading, semiotics, and poetics . . . if no one any longer asks 'What is the structure of this poem?' or 'What is the intention of the author and has it been realized?' or 'In what tradition does the poet enroll himself and with what consequences for that tradition?'" (*Correctness* 70). Of course, Fish's opinion is just Fish's opinion, as even he admits: of literary criticism and the pleasures and rewards it brings, he says, "I can't stay away from the stuff. It's what I do; and that, finally, is the only justification I can offer for its practice" (*Correctness* 112). And this justification, offered publicly in the Clarendon Lectures at Oxford University, is a cleaned-up and toned-down version of a similar point made to an audience of peers at the English Institute in 1991: "there is no justification whatsoever for [my] performance, . . . it is irresponsible, self-indulgent, self-aggrandizing, and entirely without redeeming social or intellectual value. It is just something I have always wanted to do" ("Volvos" 108).

It's true: being "irresponsible, self-indulgent, self-aggrandizing, and entirely without redeeming social or intellectual value" is a lot of fun. It is indeed "nice work if you can get it" (Fish, citing David Lodge citing George and Ira Gershwin, *Correctness* 114). The problem is getting the work, as Fish realizes, and that means offering compelling justification to "the *public,* that generalized body that wants, not unreasonably, to believe that the cultural activities it sustains have a benign relationship to its concerns and values" (*Correctness* 115–16). When many people think that relationship anything but benign, when university budgets are under attack and when trustees and legislatures demand accountability of professors, the question is this: what justification will do?

Fish rightly contests the justification offered by Robbins, Bérubé, and others: that our work is of socially redeeming value because we now study the intricacies of texts far less elite than poems—of Dolly Parton, say, or of the reinscription of gender stereotypes in the fitness competitions shown on ESPN. What Fish offers as an alternative, however, is cynical, certainly not progressive, and ultimately, I think, not even effective: we should, he argues, "hire lobbyists . . . publicity-seeking types who are always thinking of ways to grab huge hunks of newspaper space or air time and fill it with celebrations of the university so compelling that millions of Americans will go to bed thankful that the members of the Duke English Department are assuring the survival and improvement of Western civilization" (*Correctness* 126). We are to "call in a professional" to make millions of people believe that what's good for Duke's English department is good for America.

Perhaps what's good for Duke's English department is good for America, but is it good for the English department at the University of Alabama, at Fort Hays State University, or at Pima Community College? Can the English department at any of these institutions do what Duke's does—or did? What disturbs me about Fish's proposal is not just that it promotes professionalism and the cult of expertise, which I have argued contributes significantly and increasingly to inequality in this society. What also disturbs me is that, at least in *Professional Correctness,* Fish subscribes to a narrow definition of the profession and thus does not recognize that a principal threat to professional literary criticism does not come from among the critics, from new historicists and cultural materialists who engage in political criticism, but from our colleagues in composition, English as a second language, and linguistics, from, that is, a need to service ever increasing numbers of remedial and basic courses in the English language and composition.

Fish rightly argues that "when you exchange one activity for another" you are no longer doing what you did but something else; and that in the bargain, you lose something, which may be valuable. But Fish's description of what that exchange entails—cultural criticism for literary criticism, Madonna for Milton—is rarified and elitist. It is not a description that most people in the profession would recognize as applying to them. For most people in the profession, the exchange is Peter Elbow for Milton, composition for literary criticism.

Increasingly, it is the opportunity to teach all those who arrive on campus unprepared for college-level work, and it is consignment to the low end of a two-track system of professional hiring, a position from which they look with some mixture of admiration, envy, and resentment at people like Fish, or even me, who do literary and cultural criticism.

As much as I agree with Fish's analysis of the work of most cultural critics, I cannot agree that the crisis in the profession will be overcome if we all stick to close reading and then hire a lobbyist to persuade fifty state legislatures and one federal Congress that in doing so, we are saving Western civilization. The crisis in the profession is part of a crisis in our system of education, because of the role education plays in distributing economic and cultural opportunity in this society, because of the role education plays in the creation of class distinction and inequality.

Many readers, I know, remain unconvinced of this point. But many if not all of our current students believe that playing our game is "the only way to win" at life in the twenty-first century. In 1992, according to the National Center for Educational Statistics, fully 59 percent of all graduating high school seniors expected to become professionals; 84 percent expected to obtain a bachelor's degree. And the vast majority of these students hold these expectations, not because they want to think seriously about poetics or consensus historians or even statistical regression models but because they want to do well on the job market. Obviously, as Kenneth Gray and Edwin Herr point out, college is considered to be compulsory by high school students, and they think this "regardless of their abilities, academic preparation, or labor market realities" (8–9). Treating all students as if they are academically gifted—and creating in the process the notion that only such persons can obtain a well-paying job and enjoy a satisfying cultural life—sets up millions of these students for failure, for the accumulation only of huge debt and even more frustration. But "college mania" is a costly and dangerous proposition for the polity as well— in terms of federal and state subsidies, defaults on student loans, and perhaps most significantly, an inability to fill positions in skilled technical, craft, and repair work, jobs that pay well, are plentiful, and are crucial to the functioning of the economy (Gray and Herr 9–18).

In chapter 1, I followed Veblen in arguing that the academy, and in particular perhaps its humanists and artists, perpetuates the cultural structure that guarantees the "irksomeness" of labor. We thus produce "an aversion to labor" ("Labor" 201). We do this job well, so well that today, almost all high school students plan to obtain a bachelor's degree in the hope that they will not have to do irksome labor. But our success in creating these aspirations now threatens us because, for a number of familiar reasons having to do with the "egali-tarian sentiments of this country," the students' academic preparation and tal-ent increasingly fail to match their aspirations. Or as Evan Watkins puts it, just a bit differently: for public education, "the long-range 'problem' . . . was that a whole lot more people wanted to be intelligent, thought they were intelligent, and could find reasons to support a conviction of their own intelligence than a deeply stratified social organization could allow to possess the social rewards of intelligence" (74–75).

One of the readers of this manuscript, whose name I do not know, asked of me "one basic question"—"why on earth should anyone expect University professors willingly to 'reduce the power of formal education over the lives and life chances of all people'?" I think that we should do so because it would make for a better, more egalitarian society, one with less polarized political discourse and happier and more satisfied citizens. Altruism, however, is not convincing, of that I am aware. So, the bottom line is this: it is in our self-interest as a pro-fession to do so. I have argued throughout that the profession's turn to cultural politics and the breaking down of racial and gender barriers is a move that does good without threatening fundamentally the structure of the profession. Regardless of whether our profession includes women or racial minorities, or whether we write about Madonna as well as Milton, what we cannot challenge is privilege based on intellectual accomplishment and distinction. Maintaining the value of intellectual accomplishment and distinction is the limit beyond which we cannot go in promoting egalitarianism in the academy or in the pro-fession. What that limit is, I do not know—GREs of 800? 900? 1100? An inabil-ity to punctuate or to construct subordination? But as argued, status groups are predicated on exclusion. Our professional house may be big, and doubtless needed expansion and renovation, but it cannot take expansion indefinitely without suffering strain or even collapse. Brint and Krause have shown this to be the case in their studies of professional expansion in the last fifty years, and what they document is an erosion of professional group distinctiveness and power, which promises to continue.

Fish is correct: "artistic freedom is purchased at the expense of artistic efficacy" (*Correctness* 36). Robbins, Bérubé, and many others think we lack efficacy, and want more. Fish thinks we lack efficacy, but doesn't care. He is pleased, or at least accepting of the fact that "no one cares very much about lit-erary criticism outside the confines of its *professional* practice" (*Correctness* 55). But while no one cares very much about literary criticism, people do care very much about the market value of a bachelor's or professional degree, and to that extent they care very much about us and what we do. They think we are efficacious, and so do I. We have too much effect on people's lives, and our "artistic" or intellectual freedom is what is at the stake, as people and legislatures insist on better pedagogy and more teaching, because increasingly we have to do not only our own job but the job the high schools fail to do. We need to be far less important to people's lives than we are. As Gray and Herr argue, we need to develop a variety of ways to educate high school students and to prepare them to enjoy a good life, one in which, for instance, craftwork would not be considered irksome. If we cannot support and work toward such a goal for altruistic reasons, because it is right, then we should do so for the reason of our own bottom line, which is to protect our intellectual work and freedom.

Notes

Chapter 1

1. Greene's attack caused quite a stir among the literati in London, with Marlowe and Shakespeare taking great offense at the dead man's remarks. One result was a public apology to Shakespeare published later that year by Henry Chettle, who had facilitated the posthumous publication of Greene's manuscript. Scholars usually accept Chettle's apology at face value—Schoenbaum calls it a "glowing tribute" (52)—particularly since it is not partnered by an apology to Marlowe, whom Greene had criticized as an atheist and Machiavellian. Chettle avers that Shakespeare is known to be civil, upright, honest, and talented (Schoenbaum 52).

2. Livingston probably would object to my characterization of his argument, since he argues only that the "priority" of class recedes under consumer capitalism. Still, talk of the "periodization of the principle of class" (80) suggests a kind of historical movement or progression, a getting beyond or a giving way of class. Similarly, no talk of status suggests that "alternative principles of social organization such as race and gender" (78) are twentieth-century advances or innovations, when in fact stratification by status has a long history.

3. Class membership and status membership can coincide, thus offering, in Giddens's words, a situation where "structuration deriving from economic organisation 'overlaps' with, or, in Dahrendorf's terms, is 'superimposed' upon, that deriving from evaluative categorisations based upon ethnic or cultural differences. Where this is so, status group membership itself becomes a form of market capacity. Such a situation frequently offers the strongest possible source of class structuration, whereby there develop clear-cut differences in attitudes, beliefs and style of life between the classes" (112). Guillory notes a specific instance of this in modern Europe: "the humanist intellectuals of the early modern period (some of whom of course were still clergy) were conquered by the dominant bourgeois class in the later eighteenth century . . . by giving to them the important function of producing—primarily through the educational system—a cultural distinction between the bourgeoisie and the lower classes. The schools made possible a kind of mimetic identification of bourgeois culture with aristocratic

culture. The cultural distinction between classes has operated since the early modern period as a mode of ideological domination of the working class, a strategic doubling of the class hierarchy as a status hierarchy" ("Intellectuals" 134–35).

4. A note about terminology is necessary. I assume my audience is composed mostly of academics, and I know some writers distinguish between academics and intellectuals, but I use *intellectual,* as well as *professional* and *literary critics,* more often than *academic* and I do so for four reasons. First, *academic* is largely inaccurate for periods prior to the twentieth century. Second, my concern about class bias among intellectuals today is not limited to those of us working in universities, but extends to those of us working in politics and the media and even in lawyers' or physicians' offices. Third, research suggests that for the most part, the politics of academics is only marginally different from that of other professionals. The fourth reason is a matter of aesthetics: *academic* is not pleasing to my ear. Furthermore, although my target here is generally the hypocrisy or blindness of left intellectuals, who exercise power by invoking "the rhetoric of egalitarianism and anti-elitism," (Genovese 35) I modify *intellectual* by *left* only when I mean to distinguish such intellectuals from conservative intellectuals, who also suffer from class bias but do so willingly. Whether from the left or the right or even the middle, intellectuals reveal class bias, but as Eugene Genovese puts it, conservative intellectuals accept the necessity of and indeed "strongly prefer" a society "based on a hierarchy that recognizes human inequality" (27). Left intellectuals, I would like to assume, are willing to change their attitudes and behavior, given persuasive arguments and enough time.

5. A fourth institution, the church, is clearly more relevant to the sixteenth century than it is to the twentieth. In terms of managing inequality, I would judge it to be, in Raymond Williams's terms, an institution whose importance for us is residual (cf. *Marxism* 121–27).

Chapter 2

1. On education as a means of social control and its role in reproducing class distinctions, see, for example Apple; Aronowitz and Giroux; Bauman; Bernstein; Bourdieu and Passeron; Collins, *Credential;* Derber, Schwartz, and Magrass; Guillory, *Capital;* Mahaffey; Terdiman; and P. Willis. In *Work Time,* Evan Watkins points out that "schools appear the motor force where a system of class boundaries reproduces itself" (245).

2. Collins cites a number of studies to support this assertion (*Credential* 19–21). Recent arguments about the ethnic or racial bias of, for example, standardized tests thus do not go far enough in pointing out the cultural bias in the educational system.

3. Guillory points out that because of such class bias, even "the right's agenda for the university always makes room for some members of minority groups, because the right believes these self-made individuals can be assimilated to the 'caste' of all those

with an interest in preserving the rights and privileges of their acquired capital" (*Capital* 47). I think Guillory is perhaps too generous to the Left. This kind of class bias is true of the Left as well; after all, as Guillory himself points out, one of his aims in writing *Cultural Capital*, is "to make visible the relative absence of class as a working category of analysis in the canon debate" (*Capital* viii). In "liberal pluralist discourse," Guillory insists, "the category of class has been systematically repressed" (*Capital* 14). In liberal pluralist discourse, class must be repressed because it is far too dangerous to the interests of those, whether of the left or the right, involved in the canon debate—or in education, generally.

4. The ledger includes (but certainly is not limited to) work by Barker and Hulme; P. Brown; Cartelli; Frey; Greenblatt, "Curse" and *Negotiations*, 21–65, 129–63; Hawkes, *Rag* 1–26, 51–72; Orgel; and D. Pease.

5. In contrast, Felperin argues that the colonialist reading had, in fact, been in eclipse: none of the many studies of *The Tempest* produced between the late 1940s and the mid-1970s "had much to say about its social realism, profound or superficial" (171).

6. Collins points out that even in societies where capital is socialized, there remains deep occupational inequality related to credentialing. At best, socialist programs to reduce inequality typically "attack only half the problem" (*Credential* 202).

7. As an entirely unrepresentative sample of the literature on affirmative action see Richard Rodriguez's *Hunger of Memory*, Stephen L. Carter's *Reflections of an Affirmative Action Baby*, the special issue of *Representations* devoted to the topic, and Pamela Burdman's report on affirmative action at the University of California, published in *Lingua Franca*.

Chapter 3

1. Marx writes to balance the account of the bourgeois historians, who acknowledge only the emancipation from slavery or serfdom required by capitalist development:

> the historical movement which changes the producers into wage-laborers appears, on the one hand, as their emancipation from serfdom and from the fetters of the guilds, and it is this aspect of the movement which alone exists for our bourgeois historians. But, on the other hand, these newly freed men became sellers of themselves only after they had been robbed of all their own means of production, and all the guarantees of existence afforded by the old feudal arrangements. And this history, the history of their expropriation, is written in the annals of mankind in letters of blood and fire. (*Capital* 875)

In this only may I dare compare myself with Marx: I write to balance the account of many upper-middle-class literary critics, who acknowledge only "the history of . . . expropriation" (putatively) accomplished by capitalist development.

2. Max Weber defines the status order as "the way in which social honor is distributed in a community between typical groups participating in this distribution" (927 and passim). Stratification by status reveals the distribution of prestige or honor in a society.

3. Certainly debate continues in history, sociology, and literary criticism about the nature and the timing of the transition to capitalism. Suffice it to say that I find most sensible the positions of those who complicate the argument, who argue, like Fernand Braudel, that what characterizes the preindustrial economy is the coexistence of an inflexible, inert, and slow-moving primitive economy "alongside trends—limited and in the minority, yet active and powerful—that were characteristic of modern growth" (5; Wallerstein).

4. Only slightly less peculiar to the modern bourgeois is the precapitalist subordination of economics to "the real business of life, which is salvation." As R. H. Tawney explains, men and women in early modern England "inherited from the Middle Ages . . . the belief that the world of economic conduct did not form a closed compartment with laws of its own, but was amenable, like other departments of conduct, to moral criteria, the ultimate sanction of which was the authority of the Christian church" (*Usury* 107). Obviously the power of this belief was huge, and doubtless it provided (additional) ideological support for the status order I am describing in this chapter. But it is beyond this chapter's scope to address the connections between the religious order and the status order. Perhaps it is enough to note that rationalized economic activity redefined both.

5. Lisa Jardine describes the tension created by bourgeois assaults on such monopolies in discussing the flurry of Elizabethan sumptuary legislation. Intended to police the border between gentry and commoner, the legislation was doomed to failure, since "the affluent burghers with ready money to dress like the gentry were also the purveyors of the commodity being legislated about: expensive fabrics" (145).

6. See, for example, essays by Burke, *"Timon";* Chorost; Draper; Kahn; Miola; Muir; and Pettet.

7. Both Draper and Pettet think Shakespeare rather clear-headed in *Timon,* and both critics contrast it to Shakespeare's earlier consideration of the issue in *The Merchant of Venice,* where, as Walter Cohen observes, "the concluding tripartite unity of Antonio, Bassanio, and Portia enacts . . . interclass harmony between aristocratic landed wealth and mercantile capital, with the former dominant" (772). If *Merchant* suggests a fantasy reconciliation between these contrasting elites, *Timon* presents an uncompromising vision of who the losers will be in the transition from feudalism to capitalism, from a status society to a class society. As Pettet concludes, by the time he writes *Timon,* Shakespeare "appears to realize that the new anti-feudal forces of commercialism, money, and self-interest are in the ascendent" (329).

8. On the poverty and economic inequality of pre-industrial Europe, see for example, Cipolla; Clay; and Berger. On the brutality of Elizabethan and Jacobean England, see Barker.

9. For views by sociologists on the pejorative use of capitalism, see P. Berger and Wrong.

10. That limited but striking convergence is described as well by Eugene Genovese in *The Southern Tradition,* although Genovese's aim—to recuperate "the achievements of the white people of the South" for a late-twentieth-century critique of capitalism and modernization (xi)—is considerably different from Grady's.

11. Along with monopolistic market control and high social status, work autonomy is a constitutive characteristic of professional work. On this point, see Bledstein; Brint; Randall Collins; Krause; and Larson.

Chapter 4

1. So strong is this authority that in the right circumstances, even professionals themselves can be subject to it. Anthropologist Alma Gottlieb describes how during her pregnancy she became subject to professional expertise and eventually, after much effort and frustration, overcame it. Gottlieb and her husband "vowed to compel the medical system operating in our local hospital to accommodate our vision of birth" (12), which they did because they understood the protocols of expertise and could confront their "physician with a different system of authority, but one that was nonetheless premised on evidence to which he could relate. Impoverished women in inner-city hospitals do not partake of this conceptual system, and thus are not so graciously accorded the opportunities I was of recasting their birthing experiences" (13–14).

2. Edsall points out that in 1978, "Congress, for the first time since the Democratic party achieved majority status in 1932, passed an individual tax cut in which the goal of income redistribution was effectively abandoned and the centerpiece of the legislation, a cut in capital gains rates, was targeted toward the upper-middle class and the rich. The 1978 tax bill presaged, well before the election of Ronald Reagan, the new direction in tax policy, which reached full force with the enactment of the 1981 tax bill. . . . The Ninety-fifth Congress (1977–78), with overwhelming Democratic majorities in both the House and the Senate, and with a Democrat in the White House, cut the top tax rate on capital gains, a form of income earned almost exclusively by the very rich, from 48 to 28 percent, while raising the Social Security tax, which, because it is applied to the first dollar earned but exempts entirely income in excess of $37,800 as of 1984, is the most regressive federal levy" (65).

3. I am aware that in invoking capitalism here, I write in terms that are overly general. One might object, for example, that corporate capitalism is less interested in the widening of opportunities than is entrepreneurial capitalism. Perhaps; although James Livingston would not agree. Nevertheless, I am happy to concede that varieties of capitalism exist, and that some may be "better" than others. As I have argued elsewhere, all capital is not the same, yet in criticism, capital is construed as monolithic in its hegemony ("Respect").

4. Wayne explains Knights's inability to detect in Jonson's work a complicity with and celebration of commercial culture by highlighting Knights's own relationship to commercial culture. Anticipating the kind of analysis offered by Terence Hawkes in *That Shakespeherian Rag* or *Meaning by Shakespeare,* Wayne points out the historicity of Knights's intellectual and moral biases, biases that Knights shared with F. R. Leavis and others associated with *Scrutiny* in the 1930s, men who "could imagine themselves as part of an independent 'critical minority,' whose task it was to oppose the alienation of life and of language in modern commercial and industrial society by bearing witness to the moral, 'organic community' of the past" (27–28). Knights reads Jonson as a compatriot and precursor, sees him as a means to an end, an end that Jonson himself could not have imagined, according to Wayne. Capitalism

> had not yet triumphed to the point where a sufficient surplus capital existed to sustain a large-scale educational apparatus, one that could produce not only a technically trained managerial elite but a cultural elite as well who could imagine themselves to be morally superior to and independent of the new economic order. . . . Jonson could not easily blind himself to the manner in which his claim to special status was dependent on the emerging commodity system of economic and social exchange. (28)

5. Robert Sayre and Michael Löwy identify "the unifying element of the romantic movement . . . throughout the key European countries . . . [as an] opposition to capitalism in the name of precapitalist values" (26).

6. Some scholars, such as David Hall and Roger Chartier, have criticized Levine's nostalgic invocation of a "shared culture" in early-nineteenth-century America. But after pointing out the exclusions and social divisions within that culture, and thus rightly rejecting Levine's evolutionary model of cultural development, even his critics admit that during that century, a collision occurred between art and the market in America and Europe.

7. A selection of essays on *Coriolanus* is the following: Adelman; Bristol, "Lenten"; Burke, "Faction"; Danson; Gurr; Paster; Tennenhouse; and Zeeveld.

8. Burke continues: "Indeed, though the word 'noble' suggests to most of us either moral or social connotations, Coriolanus takes it for granted that only the socially noble can have nobility of any sort" ("Faction" 83).

9. Regarding the former approach, Cavell points out the obvious in noting that "in practice this has in recent years been psychoanalytic" (145). Bristol offers a similar breakdown of criticism on the play ("Lenten" 219–21).

10. For a model of social relations based on negotiation, see Leinwand. In *The Velvet Glove,* sociologist Mary Jackman offers a less sanguine view of negotiation, suggesting "that hostility is rarely the active ingredient of exploitative relations. The ideological pressures created by dominant groups are more likely to be subtle and insidious than blatant or hostile" (2).

11. Both Elias and Greenblatt support a historically circumscribed understanding and use of psychoanalysis. Elias sees "changes in the structure of personality" as following upon "specific changes in the structure of human relations" (*Process* 445), a conception largely supportive of Greenblatt's more specific claim that "psychoanalytic interpretation seems to follow upon rather than to explain Renaissance texts" ("Psychoanalysis" 221).

12. Elias calls the court "a kind of stock exchange" in which "an estimate of the 'value' of each individual is continuously being formed" (*Process* 476). As a result, success at court requires "a curbing of the affects in favour of calculated and finely shaded behaviour in dealing with people" (*Court* 111). Agnew discusses the affective control required for business negotiation (79–86).

13. In fairness to Bristol and to my argument as well, I must emphasize the "more or less" in the sentence cited. Bristol adds that "in itself . . . a constitution does not resolve the conflicts built into the division of social labor. Active and open conflict is suspended and deferred; sociocultural and discursive antagonism persists, however, and one or another party to the ongoing process of legitimation may at any time withhold consent." It is for these reasons, Bristol thinks, that the story of Coriolanus "retains its potentially explosive character" ("Lenten" 211)

14. Following Mark Kishlansky, both Patterson and Richard Wilson agree that what is at issue here is the replacement of selection by election within an already established system of political representation. Wilson notes: "if critics are perplexed by the status of the peoples' 'voices' in *Coriolanus* this is because the text reflects contemporary confusion about representative government" (*Power* 99). Patterson and Wilson disagree over the meaning of this bit of political evolution.

15. Bristol concurs: "Simply to say 'forbidden things' about Shakespeare or to connect his work to an ideologically subversive discourse remains bound up in the politically weak and practically insignificant corporate goal-values of pluralism unless the critique of tradition breaks out towards an active constituency" ("Lenten" 220). Bristol liked this point so well he repeated it in *Shakespeare's America, America's Shakespeare* (61).

16. Wilson suggests that Coriolanus's "tragedy . . . is that he cannot dominate the marketplace as he monopolises the field" (*Power* 97). This seems reasonable to me, if perhaps the other side of the coin I'm flipping.

17. Leading up to that statement, Homans suggests that "quite possibly, it would be appropriate for students to unionize at those schools where teaching loads are much higher than at Yale and where reliance on graduate teaching is much greater. Part-time and adjunct faculty with PhDs present an even more legitimate motive to unionize" (11). This is bizarre: does Homans actually mean to suggest that students at such schools are not in training to be professionals or that adjuncts holding the Ph.D. are not professionals? Characteristic of the debate on academic labor is an inability to distinguish between professionalization and unionization as modes of organizing for the market and thus to recognize that professionalization and unionization are not necessarily antithetical (see Parkin, Murphy, Barnes).

Chapter 5

1. This desire is not exclusively about the environment. Many migrants from California in particular wished to escape not just—or even primarily—pollution and congestion but also visible signs of poverty and race (B. Brown 14).

2. See Dennis Kennedy and Barbara Hodgdon for applications of the literature on tourism to Shakespeare. Important work on tourism includes that by James Clifford, Dean MacCannell, Valene Smith, and John Urry. Increasingly, the literature questions the usefulness of tourism as a mode of economic development in the developing world and in the deindustrializing West.

3. Jonathan Bate observes that "we are confronted for the first time in history with the possibility of there being no part of the earth left untouched by man" (56). But many social and natural scientists think we have already reached that point: concludes political scientist and ecocritic Timothy W. Luke, "Bill McKibben and Carolyn Merchant, to a very real extent, are right. Nature has ended. Nature is dead. . . . There really [are] no lands without any traces of some large social presence" (66). In a recent essay on the environmental justice movement, Lawrence Buell also arrives at this conclusion: what we have now is "the inextricable imbrication of outback with metropolis" ("Toxic" 659).

4. For a contrary view of the Romantic position on pastoral and the environment, see Bate.

5. For a report on environmental justice movements and their relationships to both mainstream environmentalism and the history of pastoralism in America, see Buell ("Toxic"). According to the past president of the Rural Sociological Society, Frederick H. Buttel, environmentalism "will probably need to be tied to social justice in order to be enduring" (16).

6. Obviously, it is beyond the scope of this chapter to deal with all or even many of the effects of land-use policy in Oregon and elsewhere in the Pacific Northwest. Many of these effects are laudable; social dislocation, I argue, is not.

7. Sturtevant reports that in the southern Oregon communities of the Applegate River watershed, both the "poverty rate, as well as the mean household and average property values, are higher than [those] of the surrounding region." Gentrification and the loss of well-paying working-class jobs has made the Applegate communities "a study in contrasts of class and lifestyle" (5).

8. Thomas Geoghegan makes a similar point: "In Tom Wolfe's *Bonfire of the Vanities,* supposed novel of our time, the hero, an investment banker, discovers the 'other class' when he takes a wrong turn and runs over a black kid in a ghetto. Imagine if Wolfe had written a novel in which an investment banker runs over a middle-aged steelworker. It would not even have occurred to Wolfe. Nor would it sell. Yet it happens every day" (215–16).

Chapter 6

1. On the Sokal affair, see Sokal, "Transgressing" and "Physicist," as well as Pollitt; Frank; E. Willis; Weinberg; and the dossier in *Social Text,* which includes commentaries by Harraway, Hirschkop, Dusek, Lindee, Lears, T. Miller, and Ross.

2. This literature is huge. See, for example, Barnes; Boggs; Croteau; Melucci; Morris and Mueller; and Alan Scott.

3. Most of these commentators imply that the social Left and its popular wing, the trade unions, were unambiguously racist, sexist, homophobic, and hostile to concerns about the environment, and thus include civil rights organizations among the new social movements. Aronowitz complicates this analysis by linking the trade unions and the civil rights organizations to the social Left. Contemporary social movements, by which he means those promoting feminism, gay rights, and environmentalism, "abandoned class politics for bad political but good historical reasons, not the least of which is the blindness, even hostility, of the trade unions and the civil rights organizations, the still largest and most influential organizations of the popular Left, to cultural issues" ("Radicalism" 85). The unions are self-interested, pressing class issues only at the bargaining table; and the civil rights organizations, "it is fair to say . . . [have] focused on pressuring large corporations and state institutions to provide mobility for its technical and professional intellectuals rather than pressing for economic policies to alleviate the startling decline of living standards for the black majority" ("Radicalism" 86).

4. I do not know whether Gans would be pleased or horrified to discover that humanists, too, endure the kinds of pressures he describes within sociology, pressures that fetishize the immediate and the recent and create an ahistoricity which, he assumes, "makes us look foolish in the eyes of the historians and other humanists" (*Sense* 298).

5. It was a generation gap that affected even, and perhaps especially radicals: in 1965 Irving Howe lamented that "a generation is missing in the life of American radicalism, the generation that would now be in its late thirties, the generation that did not show up. The result is an inordinate difficulty in communication between the young radicals and those unfortunate enough to have reached—or, God help us, even gone beyond—the age of forty" ("New" 23).

Works Cited

Abbott, Carl, Deborah Howe, and Sy Adler. Introduction. *Planning the Oregon Way: A Twenty-Year Evaluation*. Ed. Carl Abbott, Deborah Howe, and Sy Adler. Corvallis: Oregon State UP, 1994. ix–xxiv.

Adelman, Janet. "'Anger's My Meat': Feeding, Dependency, and Aggression in *Coriolanus*." *Shakespeare: Pattern of Excelling Nature*. Ed. David Bevington and Jay Halio. Newark: U of Delaware P, 1978. 108–24.

Agnew, Jean-Christophe. *Worlds Apart: The Market and the Theater in Anglo-American Thought, 1550–1750*. Cambridge: Cambridge UP, 1986.

Ahmad, Aijaz. *In Theory: Classes, Nations, Literatures*. London: Verso, 1992.

Alpers, Paul. *What Is Pastoral?* Chicago: U of Chicago P, 1996.

Antler. "Job Replacement for Loggers of Old Growth." *River Styx* 41 (1994): 28–29.

Anzaldúa, Gloria. *Borderlands/La Frontera: The New Mestiza*. San Francisco: Spinsters/aunt lute, 1987.

Appel, Libby. *Prologue*. Oregon Shakespeare Festival (spring 1996).

Appiah, K. Anthony. "Battle of the Bien-Pensant." Rev. of *Critical Condition: Feminism at the Turn of the Century*, by Susan Gubar. *New York Review of Books* 27 April 2000: 42–44.

Apple, Michael W. *Teachers and Texts: A Political Economy of Class and Gender Relations in Education*. New York: Routledge, 1988.

Ariès, Philippe. *Centuries of Childhood. A Social History of Family Life*. Trans. Robert Baldick. New York: Random House, 1962.

Armstrong, Nancy, and Leonard Tennenhouse. *The Imaginary Puritan: Literature, Intellectual Labor, and the Origins of Personal Life*. Berkeley and Los Angeles: U of California P, 1994.

Aronowitz, Stanley. *The Death and Rebirth of American Radicalism*. New York: Routledge, 1996.

———. "Toward Radicalism: The Death and Rebirth of the American Left." *Social Text* 13.3 (1995): 69–95.

Aronowitz, Stanley, and Henry A. Giroux. *Postmodern Education: Politics, Culture, and Social Criticism*. Minneapolis: U of Minnesota P, 1991.

Barber, Benjamin. *Strong Democracy: Participatory Politics for a New Age.* Berkeley and Los Angeles: U of California P, 1984.

Bari, Judi. *Timber Wars.* Monroe: Common Courage, 1994.

Barish, Jonas. *Ben Jonson and the Language of Prose Comedy.* New York: Norton, 1970.

Barker, Francis. *The Culture of Violence: Tragedy and History.* Chicago: U of Chicago P, 1993.

Barker, Francis, and Peter Hulme. "Nymphs and Reapers Heavily Vanish: The Discursive Con-texts of *The Tempest.*" *Alternative Shakespeares.* Ed. John Drakakis. London: Methuen, 1985. 191–205.

Barnes, Barry. *The Elements of Social Theory.* Princeton: Princeton UP, 1995.

Bate, Jonathan. *Romantic Ecology: Wordsworth and the Environmental Tradition.* London: Routledge, 1991.

Bauman, Zygmunt. *Memories of Class: The Pre-history and After-life of Class.* London: Routledge and Kegan Paul, 1992.

Beaty, Jack. "Who Speaks for the Middle Class?" *Atlantic Monthly* May 1994: 65–78.

Beaumont, Francis. *The Knight of the Burning Pestle.* Ed. Norman Rabkin. *Drama of the English Renaissance II: The Stuart Period.* Ed. Russell A. Fraser and Norman Rabkin. New York: Macmillan, 1976. 517–48.

Bell, Daniel. *The End of Ideology: On the Exhaustion of Political Ideas in the Fifties.* New York: Free P, 1960. With a new afterword. Cambridge: Harvard UP, 1988.

———. "Interpretations of American Politics." *The New American Right.* Ed. Daniel Bell. New York: Criterion Books, 1955. 3–32.

Bennett, Susan. *Performing Nostalgia: Shifting Shakespeare and the Contemporary Past.* London: Routledge, 1996.

Berger, Harry, Jr. *Second World and Green World: Studies in Renaissance Fiction-Making.* Berkeley and Los Angeles: U of California P, 1988.

Berger, Peter L. *The Capitalist Revolution: Fifty Propositions about Prosperity, Equality, and Liberty.* New York: Basic Books, 1986.

Bernstein, Basil. *Class, Codes, and Control.* London: Routledge, 1971.

Bérubé, Michael. *The Employment of English: Theory, Jobs, and the Future of Literary Studies.* New York: New York UP, 1998.

Beynon, Huw. "Class and Historical Explanation." *Social Orders and Social Classes in Europe since 1500: Studies in Social Stratification.*" Ed. M. L. Bush. London: Longman, 1992. 230–49.

Bledstein, Burton J. *The Culture of Professionalism: The Middle Class and the Development of Higher Education in America.* New York: Norton, 1978.

Boggs, Carl. *Social Movements and Political Power: Emerging Forms of Radicalism in the West.* Philadelphia: Temple UP, 1986.

Bond, Edward. *Edward Bond Plays: Three.* London: Methuen, 1987.

Bourdieu, Pierre. "The Corporatism of the Universal: The Role of Intellectuals in the Modern World." *Telos* 81 (1989): 99–110.

———. *Distinction: A Social Critique of the Judgement of Taste.* Trans. Richard Nice. Cambridge: Harvard UP, 1984.

Bourdieu, Pierre, and Jean-Claude Passeron. *Reproduction in Education, Society, and Culture.* Trans. Richard Nice. London: Sage, 1977.

Braudel, Fernand. *Afterthoughts on Material Civilization and Capitalism.* Baltimore: Johns Hopkins UP, 1977.

Brint, Steven. *In an Age of Experts: The Changing Role of Professionals in Politics and Public Life.* Princeton: Princeton UP, 1994.

Bristol, Michael D. *Big-Time Shakespeare.* New York: Routledge, 1997.

———. "Lenten Butchery: Legitimation Crisis in *Coriolanus*." *Shakespeare Reproduced: The Text in History and Ideology.* Ed. Jean. E. Howard and Marion F. O'Connor. New York: Methuen, 1987. 206–24.

———. *Shakespeare's America, America's Shakespeare.* New York: Routledge, 1990.

Brown, Beverly A. *In Timber Country: Working People's Stories of Environmental Conflict and Urban Flight.* Philadelphia: Temple UP, 1995.

Brown, Paul. "'This thing of darkness I acknowledge mine': *The Tempest* and the Discourse of Colonialism." *Political Shakespeare: New Essays in Cultural Materialism.* Ed. Jonathan Dollimore and Alan Sinfield. Ithaca: Cornell UP, 1985. 48–71.

Buell, Lawrence. "American Pastoral Ideology Reappraised." *American Literary History* 1 (1989): 1–29.

———. "Toxic Discourse." *Critical Inquiry* 24 (1998): 639–65.

Burdman, Pamela. "The Long Goodbye." *Lingua Franca* June–July 1997: 28–39.

Burke, Kenneth. "*Coriolanus* and the Delights of Faction." *Language as Symbolic Action: Essays on Life, Literature, and Method.* Berkeley and Los Angeles: U of California P, 1966. 81–97.

———. *The Philosophy of Literary Form: Studies in Symbolic Action.* 3d ed. Berkeley and Los Angeles: U of California P, 1973.

———. *A Rhetoric of Motives.* Berkeley and Los Angeles: U of California P, 1969.

———. "*Timon of Athens* and Misanthropic Gold." *Language as Symbolic Action: Essays on Life, Literature, and Method.* Berkeley and Los Angeles: U of California P, 1966. 115–24.

Bush, M. L. *The English Aristocracy: A Comparative Synthesis.* Manchester: Manchester UP, 1984.

Butler, Judith. "Merely Cultural." *Social Text* 15.3–4 (1997): 265–77.

Buttel, Frederick H. "Environmentalization: Origins, Processes, and Implications for Rural Social Change." *Rural Sociology* 57 (1992): 1–27.

Caesar, Terry. "On Teaching at a Second-Rate University." *South Atlantic Quarterly* 90 (1991): 449–67.

Cappello, Mary. *Night Bloom.* Boston: Beacon P, 1998.

Carey, John. *The Intellectuals and the Masses: Pride and Prejudice among the Literary Intelligentsia, 1880–1939.* New York: St. Martin's P, 1992.

Carroll, Matthew S. *Community and the Northwestern Logger: Continuities and Changes in the Era of the Spotted Owl.* Boulder: Westview P, 1995.

Carroll, William C. "'The Nursery of Beggary': Enclosure, Vagrancy, and Sedition in the Tudor-Stuart Period." *Enclosure Acts: Sexuality, Property, and Culture in Early Modern England.* Ed. Richard Burt and John Michael Archer. Ithaca: Cornell UP, 1994. 34–47.

Cartelli, Thomas. "Prospero in Africa: *The Tempest* as Colonialist Text and Pretext." *Shakespeare Reproduced: The Text in History and Ideology.* Ed. Jean E. Howard and Marion F. O'Connor. New York: Methuen, 1987. 99–115.

Carter, Dan T. *The Politics of Rage: George Wallace, the Origins of the New Conservatism, and the Transformation of American Politics.* New York: Simon and Schuster, 1995.

Carter, Stephen L. *Reflections of an Affirmative Action Baby.* New York: Basic Books, 1991.

Cavell, Stanley. *Disowning Knowledge in Six Plays of Shakespeare.* Cambridge: Cambridge UP, 1987.

Charnes, Linda. *Notorious Identity: Materializing the Subject in Shakespeare.* Cambridge: Harvard UP, 1993.

Charney, Maurice. "*Coriolanus, Timon of Athens.*" *Shakespeare: A Bibliographic Guide.* New ed. Ed. Stanley Wells. Oxford: Clarendon, 1990.

Chartier, Roger. *Forms and Meanings: Texts, Performances, and Audiences from Codex to Computer.* Philadelphia: U of Pennsylvania P, 1995.

Chorost, Michael. "Biological Finance in Shakespeare's *Timon of Athens.*" *English Literary Renaissance* 21 (1991): 349–70.

Chronicle of Higher Education. 29 August 1997.

Cipolla, Carlo M. *Before the Industrial Revolution: European Society and Economy, 1000–1700.* 3d ed. Trans. Christopher Woodall. London: Routledge, 1993.

Clay, C. G. A. *Economic Expansion and Social Change: England, 1500–1700.* 2 vols. Cambridge: Cambridge UP, 1984.

Clifford, James. *Routes: Travel and Translation in the Late Twentieth Century.* Cambridge: Harvard UP, 1997.

Cohen, Leah Hager. *Glass, Paper, Beans: Revelations on the Nature and Value of Ordinary Things.* New York: Doubleday, 1997.

Cohen, Walter. "*The Merchant of Venice* and the Possibilities of Historical Criticism." *English Literary History* 49 (1982): 765–89.

Colie, Rosalie L. *Shakespeare's Living Art.* Princeton: Princeton UP, 1974.

Collins, Randall. *Conflict Sociology: Toward an Explanatory Science.* New York: Academic P, 1975.

———. *The Credential Society: An Historical Sociology of Education and Stratification.* New York: Academic P, 1979.

———. *Weberian Sociological Theory.* Cambridge: Cambridge UP, 1986.

Collins, Robert M. "The Originality Trap: Richard Hofstadter on Populism." *Journal of American History* 76 (1989): 150–67.

Cressy, David. "Describing the Social Order of Elizabethan and Stuart England." *Literature and History* 3 (1976): 29–44.

Cronon, William. "The Trouble with Wilderness; or, Getting Back to the Wrong Nature." *Out of the Woods: Essays in Environmental History.* Ed. Char Miller and Hal Rothman. Pittsburgh: U of Pittsburgh P, 1997. 28–50.

Croteau, David. *Politics and the Class Divide: Working People and the Middle-Class Left.* Philadelphia: Temple UP, 1995.

Dahlman, Carl J. *The Open Field System and Beyond: A Property Rights Analysis of an Economic Institution.* Cambridge: Cambridge UP, 1980.

Dahrendorf, Ralf. *Class and Class Conflict in Industrial Society.* Stanford: Stanford UP, 1959.

Danson, Lawrence K. "Metonymy and Coriolanus." *Philological Quarterly* 52 (1973): 30–42.

DeMott, Benjamin. "Rediscovering Complexity." *Atlantic Monthly* September 1988: 67–74.

Derber, Charles, William Schwartz, and Yale Magrass. *Power in the Highest Degree: Professionals and the Rise of a New Mandarin Order.* New York: Oxford UP, 1990.

Derrida, Jacques. *Specters of Marx: The State of the Debt, the Work of Mourning, and the New International.* Trans. Peggy Kamuf. New York: Routledge, 1994.

Dewey, John. *Art as Experience.* 1934. New York: Putnam's, 1980.

Dietrich, William. *The Final Forest: The Battle for the Last Great Trees of the Pacific Northwest.* New York: Simon and Schuster, 1992.

Diggins, John Patrick. *The Rise and Fall of the American Left.* New York: Norton, 1992.

DiMaggio, Paul. "Cultural Boundaries and Structural Change: The Extension of the High Culture Model to Theater, Opera, and the Dance, 1900–1940." *Cultivating Differences: Symbolic Boundaries and the Making of Inequality.* Ed. Michèle Lamont and Marcel Fournier. Chicago: U of Chicago P, 1992. 21–57.

Dimock, Wai-Chee, and Michael T. Gilmore. Introduction. *Rethinking Class: Literary Studies and Social Formations.* Ed. Wai-Chee Dimock and Michael T. Gilmore. New York: Columbia UP, 1994. 1–11.

Douglas, Mary. Foreword. *The Gift: The Form and Reason for Exchange in Archaic Societies.* Marcel Mauss. Trans. W. D. Halls. London: Routledge, 1990. vii–xvii.

Draper, John W. "The Theme of *Timon of Athens.*" *Modern Language Review* 29 (1934): 20–31.

Dusek, Val. "Philosophy of Math and Physics in the Sokal Affair." *Social Text* 15.1 (1997): 135–38.

Eakin, Emily. "Walking the Line." *Lingua Franca* March–April 1996: 52–60.

Edsall, Thomas Byrne. *The New Politics of Inequality.* New York: Norton, 1984.

Edsall, Thomas Byrne, and Mary Edsall. *Chain Reaction: The Impact of Race, Rights, and Taxes on American Politics.* New York: Norton, 1991.

Ehrenreich, Barbara, and John Ehrenreich. "The Professional-Managerial Class." *Between Labor and Capital.* Ed. Pat Walker. Boston: South End P, 1979. 5–45.

Elias, Norbert. *The Civilizing Process: The History of Manners and State Formation and Civilization.* Trans. Edmund Jephcott. Oxford: Blackwell, 1994.

———. *The Court Society.* Trans. Edmund Jephcott. Oxford: Basil Blackwell, 1983.

Empson, William. *Some Versions of Pastoral.* New York: New Directions, 1974.

Ernaux, Annie. *Cleaned Out.* Trans. Carol Sanders. Elmwood Park: Dalkey Archive P, 1990.

Felperin, Howard. *The Uses of the Canon: Elizabethan Literature and Contemporary Theory.* Oxford: Clarendon, 1990.

Fernández-Retamar, Roberto. *Caliban and Other Essays.* Trans. Edward Baker. Minneapolis: U of Minnesota P, 1989.

Fiedler, Leslie A. *The Stranger in Shakespeare.* New York: Stein and Day, 1973.

Fischer, Claude S., et al. *Inequality by Design: Cracking the Bell Curve Myth.* Princeton: Princeton UP, 1996.

Fish, Stanley. *Professional Correctness: Literary Studies and Social Change.* Oxford: Clarendon, 1995.

———. "The Unbearable Ugliness of Volvos." *English Inside and Out: The Places of Literary Criticism.* Ed. Susan Gubar and Jonathan Kamholtz. New York: Routledge, 1993. 102–8.

Foner, Eric. "The Education of Richard Hofstadter." *Nation* 4 May 1992: 597–603.

Frank, Tom. "Textual Reckoning." *In These Times* 27 May 1996: 22–24.

Fraser, Nancy. "Heterosexism, Misrecognition, and Capitalism: A Response to Judith Butler." *Social Text* 15.3–4 (1997): 279–89.

———. *Justice Interruptus: Critical Reflections on the "Postsocialist" Condition.* New York: Routledge, 1997.

Frey, Charles. "*The Tempest* and the New World." *Shakespeare Quarterly* 30 (1979): 29–41.

Frow, John. *Cultural Studies and Cultural Value.* Oxford: Clarendon, 1995.

Gans, Eric. *Originary Thinking: Elements of a Generative Anthropology.* Stanford: Stanford UP, 1993.

Gans, Herbert J. "American Popular Culture and High Culture in a Changing Class Structure." *Prospects.* Vol. 10. Ed. Jack Salzman. New York: Cambridge UP, 1985. 17–37.

———. *Making Sense of America: Sociological Analyses and Essays.* Lanham, Md.: Rowman and Littlefield, 1999.

Genovese, Eugene D. *The Southern Tradition: The Achievement and Limitations of an American Conservatism.* Cambridge: Harvard UP, 1994.

Geoghegan, Thomas. *Which Side Are You On? Trying to Be for Labor When It's Flat on Its Back.* New York: Penguin, 1992.

Gerth, H. H., and C. Wright Mills. Introduction. *From Max Weber: Essays in Sociology.* Trans. and ed. H. H. Gerth and C. Wright Mills. 1946. New York: Oxford UP, 1974. 3–74.

Giddens, Anthony. *The Class Structure of the Advanced Societies.* New York: Harper and Row, 1973.

Gitlin, Todd. *The Sixties: Years of Hope, Days of Rage.* New York: Bantam Books, 1987.

———. *The Twilight of Common Dreams: Why America Is Wracked by Culture Wars.* New York: Henry Holt, 1995.

Gottlieb, Alma. "The Anthropologist as Mother: Reflections on Childbirth Observed and Childbirth Experienced." *Anthropology Today* 11.3 (1995): 10–14.

Gouldner, Alvin. *The Future of Intellectuals and the Rise of the New Class.* New York: Seabury P, 1979.

Grady, Hugh. *The Modernist Shakespeare: Critical Texts in a Material World.* Oxford: Clarendon, 1991.

Grafton, Anthony, and Lisa Jardine. *From Humanism to the Humanities: Education and the Liberal Arts in Fifteenth- and Sixteenth-Century Europe.* Cambridge: Harvard UP, 1986.

Gray, Kenneth C., and Edwin L. Herr. *Other Ways to Win: Creating Alternatives for High School Graduates.* Thousand Oaks, Calif.: Corwin P, 1995.

Greenblatt, Stephen. "Learning to Curse: Aspects of Linguistic Colonialism in the Sixteenth Century." *First Images of America: The Impact of the New World on the Old.* Ed. Fred Chiapelli. Berkeley and Los Angeles: U of California P, 1976. 561–80.

———. "Murdering Peasants: Status, Genre, and the Representation of Rebellion." *Representing the English Renaissance.* Ed. Stephen Greenblatt. Berkeley and Los Angeles: U of California P, 1988. 1–29.

———. "Psychoanalysis and Renaissance Culture." *Literary Theory/Renaissance Texts.* Ed. Patricia Parker and David Quint. Baltimore: Johns Hopkins UP, 1986. 210–24.

———. *Shakespearean Negotiations: The Circulation of Social Energy in Renaissance England.* Berkeley and Los Angeles: U of California P, 1988.

Greenblatt, Stephen, et al., eds. *The Norton Shakespeare: Based on the Oxford Edition.* New York: Norton, 1997.

Guillory, John. *Cultural Capital: The Problem of Literary Canon Formation.* Chicago: U of Chicago P, 1993.

———. "Literary Critics as Intellectuals: Class Analysis and the Crisis of the Humanities." *Rethinking Class: Literary Studies and Social Formations.* Ed. Wai-Chee Dimock and Michael T. Gilmore. New York: Columbia UP, 1994. 107–49.

———. "Preprofessionalism: What Graduate Students Want." *Profession 1996:* 91–99.

Gurr, Andrew. "Coriolanus and the Body Politic." *Shakespeare Survey* 28 (1975): 63–69.

Hacker, Andrew. "The Rebelling Young Scholars." *Commentary* 30 (1960): 404–12.

Hall, David D. "A World Turned Upside Down?" *Reviews in American History* 18 (1990): 10–14.

Hall, John R. "The Capital(s) of Cultures: A Nonholistic Approach to Status Situations, Class, Gender, and Ethnicity." *Cultivating Differences: Symbolic Boundaries and the Making of Inequality.* Ed. Michèle Lamont and Marcel Fournier. Chicago: U of Chicago P, 1992. 257–85.

Halpern, Richard. "'The picture of Nobody': White Cannibalism in *The Tempest*." *The Production of English Renaissance Culture*. Ed. David Lee Miller, Sharon O'Dair, and Harold Weber. Ithaca: Cornell UP, 1994. 262–92.

———. *The Poetics of Primitive Accumulation: English Renaissance Culture and the Genealogy of Capital*. Ithaca: Cornell UP, 1991.

———. *Shakespeare among the Moderns*. Ithaca: Cornell UP, 1997.

Hammond, J. R. "Working Man." *President Clinton and the Working Man*. Montgomery: Black Belt P, 1994.

Harraway, Donna. "Enlightenment@science_wars.com: A Personal Reflection on Love and War." *Social Text* 15.1 (1997): 123–29.

Harrington, Michael. "The Mystical Militants." *Beyond the New Left*. Ed. Irving Howe. New York: McCall, 1970. 33–39.

Haskell, Thomas L. "Professionalism *versus* Capitalism: R. H. Tawney, Emile Durkheim, and C. S. Peirce on the Disinterestedness of Professional Communities." *The Authority of Experts: Studies in History and Theory*. Ed. Thomas L. Haskell. Bloomington: Indiana UP, 1984. 180–225.

Hawkes, Terence. *Meaning by Shakespeare*. London: Routledge, 1992.

———. *That Shakespearian Rag: Essays on a Critical Practice*. New York: Methuen, 1986.

Hazlitt, William. *The Complete Works of William Hazlitt*. Ed. P. P. Howe. Vol. 4. London: Dent, 1930.

Herman, Jan. "Grove Theatre's Supporting Cast: Enter the Philistines." *Los Angeles Times* 31 May 1988, Orange County ed.: VI.9.

Higham, John. "The Cult of the 'American Consensus.'" *Commentary* 27 (1959): 93–100.

Hirschkop, Ken. "Cultural Studies and Its Discontents: A Comment on the Sokal Affair." *Social Text* 15.1 (1997): 131–33.

Hodgdon, Barbara. *The Shakespeare Trade: Performances and Appropriations*. Philadelphia: U of Pennsylvania P, 1998.

Hoffman, Lily M. *The Politics of Knowledge: Activist Movements in Medicine and Planning*. Albany: State UP of New York, 1989.

Hofstadter, Richard. *Anti-intellectualism in American Life*. New York: Knopf, 1969.

———. "Pseudo-Conservatism Revisited: A Postscript (1962)." *The Radical Right: The New American Right Expanded and Updated*. Garden City: Anchor Books, 1964. 97–103.

———. "The Pseudo-Conservative Revolt." *The New American Right*. Ed. Daniel Bell. New York: Criterion Books, 1955. 33–55.

Homans, Margaret. "Letter to the MLA Executive Director." Solicitation of members' comments by the MLA, 9 February 1996.

Howe, Irving. Introduction. *Beyond the New Left*. Ed. Irving Howe. New York: McCall, 1970. 3–15.

———. "New Styles in 'Leftism.'" *Beyond the New Left*. Ed. Irving Howe. New York: McCall Publishing, 1970. 19–32.

Jackman, Mary R. *The Velvet Glove: Paternalism and Conflict in Gender, Class, and Race Relations.* Berkeley and Los Angeles: U of California P, 1994.

Jacoby, Russell. *Dogmatic Wisdom: How the Culture Wars Divert Education and Distract America.* New York: Anchor, 1994.

Jameson, Fredric. *The Ideologies of Theory: Essays, 1971–1986.* Vol. 2: *The Syntax of History.* Minneapolis: U of Minnesota P, 1988.

Jardine, Lisa. *Still Harping on Daughters: Women in Seventeenth Century Drama.* Sussex: Harvester P, 1983.

Jed, Stephanie H. *Chaste Thinking: The Rape of Lucretia and the Birth of Humanism.* Bloomington: Indiana UP, 1989.

Jonson, Ben. *Bartholomew Fair.* Ed Norman Rabkin. *Drama of the English Renaissance II: The Stuart Period.* Ed. Russell A. Fraser and Norman Rabkin. New York: Macmillan, 1976. 191–239.

Kahn, Coppélia. "'Magic of Bounty': *Timon of Athens,* Jacobean Patronage, and Maternal Power." *Shakespeare Quarterly* 38 (1987): 34–57.

Karabel, Jerome, et. al. *Freshman Admissions at Berkeley: A Policy for the 1990s and Beyond.* Report by the Committee on Admissions and Enrollment. Berkeley Division, Academic Senate of the University of California. May 1989.

Karen, David. "The Politics of Class, Race, and Gender: Access to Higher Education in the United States, 1960–1986." *American Journal of Education* 99 (1991): 208–37.

Kastan, David Scott. "Is There a Class in This (Shakespearean) Text?" *Renaissance Drama.* New Series 24. Ed. Mary Beth Rose. Evanston: Northwestern UP and Newberry Library Center for Renaissance Studies, 1993. 101–21.

Kavanagh, James H. "Shakespeare in Ideology." *Alternative Shakespeares.* Ed. John Drakakis. New York: Methuen, 1985. 144–65.

Kendall, Gerald Dale. "Friend or Foe: 1000 Friends of Oregon versus Land Conservation and Development Commission (Lane County)." Master's thesis. University of Oregon. 1989.

Kendrick, Christopher. "Agons of the Manor: Symbolic Responses to the Entrenchment of Agrarian Capitalism." *The Production of English Renaissance Culture.* Ed. David Lee Miller, Sharon O'Dair, and Harold Weber. Ithaca: Cornell UP, 1994. 13–55.

Kennedy, Dennis. "Shakespeare and Cultural Tourism." *Theatre Journal* 50 (1998): 175–88.

Konrád, George, and Ivan Szelényi. *The Intellectuals on the Road to Class Power.* Trans. Andrew Arato and Richard E. Allen. New York: Harcourt Brace Jovanovich, 1979.

Kraus, Maribeth T. Letter to Janet Zandy, 1 June 1993.

Krause, Elliot A. *Death of the Guilds: Professions, States, and the Advance of Capitalism, 1930 to the Present.* New Haven: Yale UP, 1996.

Knights, L. C.. *Drama and Society in the Age of Jonson.* London: Chatto and Windus, 1962.

Kriesi, Hanspeter, et al. *New Social Movements in Western Europe: A Comparative Analysis.* Minneapolis: U of Minnesota P, 1995.

Laclau, Ernesto, and Chantal Mouffe. *Hegemony and Socialist Strategy: Towards a Radical Democratic Politics.* Trans. Winston Moore and Paul Cammack. London: Verso, 1985.

Larson, Magali Sarfatti. "The Production of Expertise and the Constitution of Expert Power." *The Authority of Experts: Studies in History and Theory.* Ed. Thomas L. Haskell. Bloomington: Indiana UP, 1984. 28–80.

———. *The Rise of Professionalism: A Sociological Analysis.* Berkeley and Los Angeles: U of California P, 1977.

Lasch, Christopher. *The Revolt of the Elites and the Betrayal of Democracy.* New York: Norton, 1995.

Lears, Jackson. "Reality Matters." *Social Text* 15.1 (1997): 143–45.

Leeman, Wayne A. *Oregon Land, Rural or Urban? The Struggle for Control.* Ashland: Millwright P, 1997.

Leinwand, Theodore B. "Negotiation and New Historicism" *PMLA* 105 (1990): 477–90.

Leonard, H. Jeffrey. *Managing Oregon's Growth: The Politics of Development Planning.* Washington, D.C.: Conservation Foundation, 1983.

Levine, Lawrence W. *Highbrow/Lowbrow: The Emergence of Cultural Hierarchy in America.* Cambridge: Harvard UP, 1988.

Lindee, M. Susan. "Wars of Out-Describing." *Social Text* 15.1 (1997): 139–42.

Lipset, Seymour Martin. "The Sources of the 'Radical Right.'" *The New American Right.* Ed. Daniel Bell. New York: Criterion Books, 1955. 168–233.

———. "Three Decades of the Radical Right: Coughlinites, McCarthyites, and Birchers (1962)." *The Radical Right: The New American Right Expanded and Updated.* Ed. Daniel Bell. Garden City: Anchor Books, 1964. 373–446.

Livingston, James. *Pragmatism and the Political Economy of Cultural Revolution, 1850–1940.* Chapel Hill: U of North Carolina P, 1994.

Loewenstein, Joseph. "The Script in the Marketplace." *Representing the English Renaissance.* Ed. Stephen Greenblatt. Berkeley and Los Angeles: U of California P, 1988. 265–78.

Love, Glen A. "*Et in Arcadia Ego:* Pastoral Theory Meets Ecocriticism." *Western American Literature* 27 (1992): 195–207.

Luke, Timothy W. *Ecocritique: Contesting the Politics of Nature, Economy, and Culture.* Minneapolis: U of Minnesota P, 1997.

MacCannell, Dean. *The Tourist: A New Theory of the Leisure Class.* 1976. New York: Schocken, 1989.

Macfarlane, Alan. *The Origins of English Individualism: The Family, Property, and Social Transition.* Oxford: Basil Blackwell, 1979.

MacInnes, Gordon. *Wrong for All the Right Reasons: How White Liberals Have Been Undone by Race.* New York: New York UP, 1996.

Mahaffey, Vicki. "The Case against Art: Wunderlich on Joyce." *Critical Inquiry* 17 (1991): 667–92.

Marx, Karl. *Capital: A Critique of Political Economy.* Trans. Ben Fowkes. Vol. 1. New York: Random House, 1977.

——. *Economic and Philosophic Manuscripts of 1844.* Trans. Martin Milligan. New York: International Publishers, 1964.

Marx, Leo. *The Machine in the Garden: Technology and the Pastoral Ideal in America.* London: Oxford UP, 1964.

Maus, Katherine Eisaman. *Inwardness and Theater in the English Renaissance.* Chicago: U of Chicago P, 1995.

Mauss, Marcel. *The Gift: The Form and Reason for Exchange in Archaic Societies.* Trans. W. D. Hall. London: Routledge, 1990.

May, Todd. *The Political Philosophy of Poststructuralist Anarchism.* University Park: Pennsylvania State UP, 1994.

McDonald, Russ. *The Bedford Companion to Shakespeare: An Introduction with Documents.* New York: St. Martin's P, 1996.

McLuskie, Kathleen E., and Felicity Dunsworth. "Patronage and the Economics of the Theater." *A New History of Early English Drama.* Ed. John D. Cox and David Scott Kastan. New York: Columbia UP, 1997. 423–40.

Meeker, Joseph. *The Comedy of Survival: Studies in Literary Ecology.* New York: Scribner's, 1974.

Melucci, Alberto. *Nomads of the Present: Social Movements and Individual Needs in Contemporary Society.* Philadelphia: Temple UP, 1990.

Miller, D. W. "Searching for Common Ground in the Debate over Urban Sprawl." *Chronicle of Higher Education* 21 May 1999: A15–16.

Miller, Toby. "Actually Existing Journal-ism." *Social Text* 15.1 (1997): 147–48.

Miola, Robert S. "Timon in Shakespeare's Athens." *Shakespeare Quarterly* 31 (1980): 21–30.

Mishel, Lawrence, Jared Bernstein, and John Schmitt. *The State of Working America.* 1996–97 ed. Armonk: M. E. Sharpe, 1997.

Mishel, Lawrence, and David M. Frankel. *The State of Working America.* 1990–91 ed. Armonk: M. E. Sharpe, 1991.

Modern Language Association. Mailing to members. 9 February 1996.

Moisan, Thomas. "'Knock me here soundly': Comic Misprision and Class Consciousness in Shakespeare." *Shakespeare Quarterly* 42 (1991): 276–90.

Monette, Paul. *Halfway Home.* New York: Crown, 1991.

Montrose, Louis. "Of Gentlemen and Shepherds: The Politics of Elizabethan Pastoral Form." *English Literary History* 50 (1983): 415–59.

——. *The Purpose of Playing: Shakespeare and the Cultural Politics of the Elizabethan Theatre.* Chicago: U of Chicago P, 1996.

Morris, Aldon D., and Carol McClurg Mueller. *Frontiers in Social Movement Theory.* New Haven: Yale UP, 1992.

Muir, Kenneth. "*Timon of Athens* and the Cash-Nexus." *The Singularity of Shakespeare and Other Essays.* New York: Barnes and Noble, 1977.

Murphy, Raymond. *Social Closure: The Theory of Monopolization and Exclusion.* Oxford: Clarendon, 1988.

Nelson, Cary, ed. *Will Teach for Food: Academic Labor in Crisis.* Minneapolis: U of Minnesota P, 1997.

Nixon, Rob. "Caribbean and African Appropriations of *The Tempest.*" *Critical Inquiry* 13 (1987): 557–78.

O'Dair, Sharon. "Freeloading Off the Social Sciences." *Philosophy and Literature* 15 (1991): 260–67.

———. "Stars, Tenure, and the Death of Ambition." *Michigan Quarterly Review* 36 (1997): 607–27.

———. "Still No Respect: Capitalism and the Cultural Choices of the Working-Class." *symplokē* 2 (1994): 159–76.

———. "Theorizing as Defeatism: A Pragmatic Defense of Agency." *Mosaic* 26.2 (1993): 111–21.

Ohmann, Richard. *English in America: A Radical View of the Profession.* 1976. Hanover: UP of New England, 1996.

———. "On PC and Related Matters." *PC Wars: Politics and Theory in the Academy.* Ed. Jeffrey Williams. New York: Routledge, 1995. 11–21.

Opotow, Susan. "Moral Exclusion and Injustice: An Introduction." *Journal of Social Issues* 46.1 (1990): 1–20.

"The Oregon Shakespeare Festival." *Oregon Shakespeare Festival.* 25 April 2000. www.starfish.com/shakespeare/theatre/osf.html.

Orgel, Stephen. "Shakespeare and the Cannibals." *Cannibals, Witches, and Divorce: Estranging the Renaissance.* Ed. Marjorie Garber. Baltimore: Johns Hopkins UP, 1987. 40–66.

Palmaffey, Tyce. "Class Struggle." *New Republic* 7 June 1999: 17–20.

Palumbo-Liu, David. "Awful Patriotism: Richard Rorty and the Politics of Knowing." Rev. of *Achieving Our Country: Leftist Thought in Twentieth-Century America,* by Richard Rorty. *Diacritics* 29.1 (1999): 37–56.

Parkin, Frank. *Marxism and Class Theory: A Bourgeois Critique.* New York: Columbia UP, 1979.

Parsons, Talcott. "Social Strains in America." *The New American Right.* Ed. Daniel Bell. New York: Criterion Books, 1955. 117–40.

———. "Social Strains in America: A Postscript (1962). *The Radical Right: The New American Right Expanded and Updated.* Ed. Daniel Bell. Garden City, N.Y.: Anchor Books, 1964. 231–38.

Paster, Gail Kern. "To Starve with Feeding: The City in *Coriolanus.*" *Shakespeare Studies* 11 (1981): 135–43.

Patterson, Annabel. *Pastoral and Ideology: Virgil to Valéry.* Berkeley and Los Angeles: U of California P, 1987.

———. *Shakespeare and the Popular Voice.* Cambridge, Mass.: Basil Blackwell, 1989.

————. "To the MLA Executive Director." Solicitation of members' comments by the MLA, 9 February 1996.

Pease, Donald. "Toward a Sociology of Literary Knowledge: Greenblatt, Colonialism, and the New Historicism." *Consequences of Theory.* Ed. Jonathan Arac and Barbara Johnson. Baltimore: Johns Hopkins U P, 1991. 108–53.

Pease, James R. "Oregon Rural Land Use: Policy and Practices." *Planning the Oregon Way: A Twenty-Year Evaluation.* Ed. Carol Abbott, Deborah Howe, and Sy Adler. Corvallis: Oregon State UP, 1994. 163–88.

Perloff, Marjorie. "An Intellectual Impasse." *Salmagundi* 72 (1986): 125–30.

Petroff, Vic. *Implementing the LCDC Goals and Guidelines: High Hopes, Painful Realities.* Boulder: Western Interstate Commission for Higher Education, 1975.

Pettet, E. C. "*Timon of Athens:* The Disruption of Feudal Morality." *Review of English Studies* 23 (1947): 321–36.

Pollitt, Katha. "Pomolotov Cocktail." *Nation* 10 June 1996: 9.

Potter, David M. "The Politics of Status." *New Leader* 24 June 1963: 26–27.

Quinn, Beth. "A tempest brews between Ashland and its Shakespeare." *Oregonian* 13 September 1999. www.oregonlive.com/news/99/09/st091301.html.

————. "Theater plan allays Ashland concern." *Oregonian* 7 October 1999. www.oregonlive.com/news/99/10/st100720.html.

Raphael, Ray. *More Tree Talk: The People, Politics, and Economics of Timber.* Washington, D.C.: Island P, 1994.

Readings, Bill. Rev. of *Cultural Capital: The Problem of Literary Canon Formation,* by John Guillory. *Modern Language Quarterly* 55 (1994): 321–26.

Representations 55 (summer 1996).

Riesman, David, and Nathan Glazer. "The Intellectuals and the Discontented Classes." *The New American Right.* Ed. Daniel Bell. New York: Criterion Books, 1955. 56–90.

Robbins, Bruce. "Oppositional Professionals: Theory and the Narratives of Professionalization." *Consequences of Theory.* Ed. Jonathan Arac and Barbara Johnson. Baltimore: Johns Hopkins UP, 1991. 1–21.

————. "The Professional-Managerial Class Revisited: An Interview with Barbara Ehrenreich." *Intellectuals: Aesthetics Politics Academics.* Ed. Bruce Robbins. Minneapolis: U of Minnesota P, 1990. 173–85.

————. "'Real Politics' and the Canon Debate." Rev. of *Marginal Forces/Cultural Centers: Tolson, Pynchon, and the Politics of the Canon,* by Michael Bérubé, and *Cultural Capital: The Problem of Literary Canon Formation,* by John Guillory. *Contemporary Literature* 35 (1994): 365–75.

————. *Secular Vocations: Intellectuals, Professionalism, Culture.* London: Verso, 1993.

Rodriguez, Richard. *Hunger of Memory: The Education of Richard Rodriguez.* Boston: Godine, 1981.

Rorty, Richard. *Achieving Our Country: Leftist Thought in Twentieth-Century America.* Cambridge: Harvard UP, 1998.

Roskelly, Hephzibah. "Telling Tales in School: A Redneck Daughter in the Academy."

Working-Class Women in the Academy: Laborers in the Knowledge Factory. Ed. Michelle M. Tokarczyk and Elizabeth A. Fay. Amherst: U of Massachusetts P, 1993. 292–307.

Ross, Andrew. "Reflections on the Sokal Affair." *Social Text* 15.1 (1997): 149–52.

Rowse, A. L. *William Shakespeare: A Biography*. New York: Harper and Row, 1963.

Rubin, Lillian B. *Worlds of Pain: Life in the Working-Class Family*. 1976. New York: Basic Books, 1992.

Said, Edward W. "An Unresolved Paradox." *MLA Newsletter* 31.2 (1999): 3.

Sanchez, Marta. "Caliban: The New Latin-American Protagonist of *The Tempest*." *Diacritics* 6.1 (1976): 54–61.

Sayre, Robert, and Michael Löwy. "Figures of Romantic Anticapitalism." *Spirits of Fire: English Romantic Writers and Contemporary Historical Methods*. Ed. G. A. Rosso and Daniel P. Watkins. Rutherford, N.J.: Fairleigh Dickinson UP, 1990. 23–68.

Schama, Simon. *Landscape and Memory*. New York: Knopf, 1995.

Schoenbaum, Samuel. *Shakespeare's Lives*. New ed. Oxford: Clarendon, 1991.

Scott, Alan. *Ideology and the New Social Movements*. London: Unwin Hyman, 1990.

Scott, Joan Wallach. "The Campaign against Political Correctness: What's Really at Stake." *PC Wars: Politics and Theory in the Academy*. Ed. Jeffrey Williams. New York: Routledge, 1995. 22–43.

Shakespeare, William. *Antony and Cleopatra*. Ed. M. R. Ridley. London: Methuen, 1984.

———. *As You Like It*. Ed. Agnes Latham. New York: Routledge, 1996.

———. *Coriolanus*. Ed. P. Brockbank. New York: Routledge, 1988.

———. *Hamlet*. Ed. H. Jenkins. New York: Methuen, 1982.

———. *King Lear*. Ed. Kenneth Muir. New York: Methuen, 1986.

———. *Macbeth*. Ed. Kenneth Muir. London: Methuen, 1986.

———. *A Midsummer Night's Dream*. Ed. Harold F. Brooks. New York: Routledge, 1979.

———. *Othello*. Ed. M. R. Ridley. New York: Methuen, 1986.

———. *The Tempest*. Ed. Frank Kermode. New York: Methuen, 1986.

———. *Timon of Athens*. Ed. H. J. Oliver. New York: Routledge, 1991.

Simpson, David. *The Academic Postmodern and the Rule of Literature: A Report on Half-Knowledge*. Chicago: U of Chicago P, 1995.

Singal, Daniel Joseph. "Beyond Consensus: Richard Hofstadter and American Historiography." *American Historical Review* 89 (1984): 976–1004.

Sleeper, Jim. *The Closest of Strangers: Liberalism and the Politics of Race in New York*. New York: Norton, 1990.

Smith, Bruce R. *Roasting the Swan of Avon: Shakespeare's Redoubtable Enemies and Dubious Friends*. Washington, D.C.: Folger Shakespeare Library, 1994.

Smith, Thomas. *De Republica Anglorum*. Ed. Mary Dewar. Cambridge: Cambridge UP, 1982.

Smith, Valene, ed. *Hosts and Guests: The Anthropology of Tourism*. Philadelphia: U of Pennsylvania P, 1977.

Snow, Donald. "Wise Use and the West's Sentimental Economy." *Writers on the Range.* Ed. Karl Hess Jr. and John A. Baden. Niwot: UP of Colorado, 1998. 27–36.

Sokal, Alan D. "A Physicist Experiments with Cultural Studies." *Lingua Franca* May–June 1996: 62–64.

———. "Transgressing the Boundaries: Toward a Transformative Hermeneutics of Quantum Gravity." *Social Text* 14.1–2 (1996): 217–52.

Stallybrass, Peter. "Worn Worlds: Clothes and Identity on the Renaissance Stage." *Subject and Object in Renaissance Culture.* Ed. Margreta de Grazia, Maureen Quilligan, and Peter Stallybrass. Cambridge: Cambridge UP, 1996. 289–320.

Stallybrass, Peter, and Allon White. *The Politics and Poetics of Transgression.* Ithaca: Cornell UP, 1986.

Steedman, Carolyn Kay. *Landscape for a Good Woman: A Story of Two Lives.* New Brunswick, N.J.: Rutgers UP, 1987.

Stone, Lawrence. *The Crisis of the Aristocracy, 1558–1641.* Abridged ed. London: Oxford UP, 1967.

Sturtevant, Victoria E. "Reciprocity of Social Capital and Collective Action." Unpublished ms. Southern Oregon State University. 1999.

Tawney, R. H. *The Agrarian Problem of the Sixteenth Century.* London: Longmans, Green, 1912.

———. Introduction. *A Discourse upon Usury.* 1572. By Thomas Wilson. Reprints of Economic Classics. New York: Augustus M. Kelley, 1965. 1–172.

Tennenhouse, Leonard. "*Coriolanus:* History and the Crisis of Semantic Order." *Comparative Drama* 10 (1976): 328–46.

Terdiman, Richard. "Is There Class in This Class?" *The New Historicism.* Ed. H. Aram Veeser. New York: Routledge, 1989. 225–42.

Thirsk, Joan. *Tudor Enclosures.* 1958. London: Historical Association, 1970.

Thomas, Keith. *Man and the Natural World: Changing Attitudes in England, 1500–1800.* London: Allen Lane, 1983.

Tomasky, Michael. *Left for Dead: The Life, Death, and Possible Resurrection of Progressive Politics in America.* New York: Free P, 1996.

Tompkins, Jane. *Sensational Designs: The Cultural Work of American Fiction.* New York: Oxford UP, 1985.

Treiman, Donald J. *Occupational Prestige in Comparative Perspective.* New York: Academic P, 1977.

Urry, John. *The Tourist Gaze: Leisure and Travel in Contemporary Societies.* London: Sage, 1990.

Veblen, Thorstein. "The Instinct of Workmanship and the Irksomeness of Labor." *American Journal of Sociology* 4 (1898): 187–201.

———. *The Theory of the Leisure Class: An Economic Study of Institutions.* New York: Modern Library, 1934.

Waldie, D. J. "The Myth of the L.A. River." *Buzz* April 1996: 80–85, 115–16.

Wallerstein, Immanuel. *The Modern World System.* New York: Academic P, 1974.

Walter, John. "A 'Rising of the People'?: The Oxfordshire Rising of 1596." *Past and Present* 107 (1985): 90–143.

Watkins, Evan. "Intellectual Work and Pedagogical Circulation in English." *Theory/Pedagogy/Politics.* Ed. Donald Morton and Mas'ud Zavarzadeh. Urbana: U of Illinois P, 1991. 201–21.

———. *Throwaways: Work Culture and Consumer Education.* Stanford: Stanford UP, 1993.

———. *Work Time: English Departments and the Circulation of Cultural Value.* Stanford: Stanford UP, 1989.

Wayne, Don E., "Drama and Society in the Age of Jonson: Shifting Grounds of Authority and Judgment in Three Major Comedies." *Renaissance Drama as Cultural History: Essays from "Renaissance Drama," 1977–1987.* Ed. Mary Beth Rose. Evanston: Northwestern UP and Newberry Center for Renaissance Studies, 1990. 3–29.

Weber, Max. *Economy and Society: An Outline of Interpretive Sociology.* 2 vols. Ed. Guenther Roth and Claus Wittich. Trans. Ephraim Fischoff, Hans Gerth, A. M. Henderson, Ferdinand Kolegar, C. Wright Mills, Talcott Parsons, Max Rheinstein, Guenther Roth, Edward Shils, and Claus Wittich. New York: Bedminster P, 1968.

Weinberg, Steven. "Sokal's Hoax." *New York Review of Books* 8 August 1996: 11–15.

Westin, Alan F. "The John Birch Society (1962)." *The Radical Right: The New American Right Expanded and Updated.* Ed. Daniel Bell. Garden City, N.Y.: Anchor Books, 1964. 239–68.

Williams, Kevin, and Victoria E. Sturtevant. "Individual Adaptation to Changes in Forest Policy and the Timber Industry: Exploratory Case Studies in Two Small Timber Communities in Southwest Oregon." Unpublished ms. Southern Oregon State University, 1999.

Williams, Raymond. *The Country and the City.* New York: Oxford UP, 1973.

———. *Culture and Society: 1780–1950.* New York: Columbia UP, 1983.

———. *Marxism and Literature.* Oxford: Oxford UP, 1977.

———. *Resources of Hope: Culture, Democracy, Socialism.* Ed. Robin Gable. London: Verso, 1989.

Willis, Deborah. "Shakespeare's *Tempest* and the Discourse of Colonialism." *Studies in English Literature* 29 (1989): 277–89.

Willis, Ellen. "My Sokaled Life." *Village Voice* 25 June 1996: 22–23.

Willis, Paul. *Learning to Labor: How Working Class Kids Get Working Class Jobs.* New York: Columbia UP, 1981.

Wilson, Luke. "Promissory Performances." *Renaissance Drama.* New Series 25. Ed. Frances E. Dolan. Evanston: Northwestern UP and Newberry Center for Renaissance Studies, 1994. 59–87.

Wilson, Richard. "Voyage to Tunis: New History and the Old World of *The Tempest.*" *English Literary History* 64 (1997): 333–57.

———. *Will Power: Essays on Shakespearean Authority.* Detroit: Wayne State UP, 1993.

Woodmansee, Martha. *The Author, Art, and the Market: Rereading the History of Aesthetics.* New York: Columbia UP, 1994.

Woronicz, Henry. "Unabashed Humanity." *Playbill* (Oregon Shakespeare Festival) 2 (1995): 2.

Wray, Matt, and Annalee Newitz, ed. *White Trash: Race and Class in America.* New York: Routledge, 1997.

Wright, Erik Olin. *Class Structure and Income Distribution.* New York: Academic P, 1979.

Wrightson, Keith. "The Social Order of Early Modern England: Three Approaches." *The World We Have Gained: Histories of Population and Social Structure.* Ed. Lloyd Bonfield, Richard M. Smith, and Keith Wrightson. Oxford: Basil Blackwell, 1986. 177–202.

Writer's Chronicle. 31.2 (1999).

Wrong, Dennis. "Disaggregating the Idea of Capitalism." *Theory, Culture, and Society* 9 (1992): 147–58.

Young, David. *The Heart's Forest: A Study of Shakespeare's Pastoral Plays.* New Haven: Yale UP, 1972.

Zeeveld, Gordon W. "*Coriolanus* and Jacobean Politics." *Modern Language Review* 57 (1962): 321–34.

Index